Killer Recipes

D1251580

Edited and Compiled by
Susan Whitfield

L & L Dreamspell
Spring, Texas

Cover and Interior Design by L & L Dreamspell

All proceeds from book sales will be donated to The American Cancer Society

ISBN: 978-1-60318-350-5

Visit us on the web at www.lldreamspell.com

Published by L & L Dreamspell
Printed in the United States of America

Contents

Breads and Breakfasts to Die For

Criminal Bites, Dips, and Beverages

Devilish Desserts

Insane Soups, Salads, and Sauces

Shameless Sides

Slayer Casseroles

Suck-ulent Main Dishes

Unlawful Vegetables

This book is dedicated to my grandson
Caleb Graham Whitfield
who is a cancer survivor, and to all others
who have been touched by cancer.

Mystery Writer Susan Whitfield's *Killer Recipes* is a collection of real family recipes, not only from her kitchen, but also those of other mystery writers. Some selected recipes they think their main characters would enjoy. All recipes included in this volume were submitted by writers and used with permission.

Please note:
Some recipes have fun, deadly names,
but all are harmless and delicious!

Breads and Breakfasts to Die For

BREAKFAST
BEFORE MAYHEM

Bishop's Bread

Preheat oven to 350° F. Grease and flour a 9"x12" pan.

Ingredients:

2 ½ cups flour
¾ cup white sugar
1 cup brown sugar
2/3 cup vegetable oil
1 egg
1 cup sour milk
1 Tbsp baking soda

Mix flour and sugars in a large bowl. Add vegetable oil and mix. Take out ½ cup for topping. Add to first mixture:
1 egg
1 cup sour milk

Mix well, then stir in 1 Tbsp baking soda dissolved in 1 Tbsp boiling water. Crumble topping evenly. Bake at 350° F for 35 minutes.

Laura DiSilverio, author of *Swift Justice*.
www.lauradisilverio.com

Bourekas de Spinaka y Kezo

In Sephardic tradition, this food is called "Desayuno," or breakfast. However, it may be eaten at any time of day. Bourekas are one of the most beloved foods for anyone who has been raised within the Judeo-Spanish culture, and are a fast favorite for friends who have the good fortune to try them.

Make the massa (dough):

2 cups of unbleached white flour
1 tsp of salt
1 tsp of dried oregano
1 tsp of dried rosemary
½ cup of water
½ cup of olive oil

Mix ingredients and let sit in refrigerator for 15 minutes. If it is too dry to roll into balls, add a little water. If it is too sticky, add some flour. If you want a flakier crust, add in a couple of tablespoons of vegetable shortening.

Make the gomo (filling):

Steam 2 packages of frozen spinach. Let cool.
When cool, add:
2 packages of farmer cheese
16 oz of feta cheese
½ a sautéed onion (optional)
6 oz of chopped kashkaval (kasseri) cheese (option for a richer, slightly gamey flavor)

Roll the dough into walnut-sized balls. Flatten them out on a cutting board. Put in a Tbsp of the gomo and then fold over so you have created a crescent. Flute the edges. Brush the top with beaten egg, and sprinkle with sesame seeds.

Spray a cookie pan with oil, and fill the pan with raw bourekas.

Put into a preheated 450° F oven.

Bake until the top just begins to tan. It should not become brown. Stick a fork in one to make sure it is cooked through. Cool and refrigerate. Heat them up in a toaster oven before eating them.

Allan W. Azouz, author of *Shadows of Souls*.
www.lldreamspell.com

Bread Machine Finnish Limpa

Ingredients:

Wet:
1 cup water
½ cup buttermilk
1/3 cup molasses
1 ½ Tbsp melted butter

Dry:
2 ¾ cups white bread flour
1 cup medium rye flour
½ cup dark, stone-ground rye flour
1 Tbsp wheat gluten
1 Tbsp dark brown sugar
1 ½ tsp salt
1 scant tsp anise seeds
2 ¼ Tbsp yeast

Place all wet ingredients in bread machine. Add all dry ingredients except yeast. Do NOT mix. Make a small depression in the dry ingredients and place the yeast in this depression. Do NOT mix.

Place mixing insert into bread machine. Close. Program for whole wheat (usually 3 hours and 40 minutes). Program crust for light. Turn on. Bread will probably be done with approximately 10 minutes left on the cycle. The recipe makes a big loaf.

Note: My machine is not programmable except by using the set cycles. If you can custom set yours for the baking cycle give it 1 hour and 30 minutes. I have no idea how this recipe works if made by hand. This is my combo for bread machine Limpa because I couldn't find one—and Finnish Limpa is truly a bread to die for.

Jane Toombs, author of *Null and Void* and *Nightingale Man*.
www.janetoombs.com

Breakfast Before Mayhem

Ingredients:

1 pound sausage, cooked and drained
6 eggs
2 cups milk
1 tsp dry mustard
1 tsp salt
2 slices white bread, cubed
1 cup grated cheddar cheese
1 onion, chopped and sautéed
1 green or red pepper, chopped
8 oz fresh or canned mushrooms

Beat eggs, milk, salt, and mustard.
Layer: bread cubes, sausage, cheese with sautéed onions, green peppers, and mushrooms.
Pour egg mixture over all in a 9" x 13" pan.
Better if made the day before serving.
Bake 40 minutes at 350° F. Serves 6.

Betty Gordon, author of *Deceptive Clarity, Murder in the Third Person*, and the short stories *Dead By Breakfast, Anna Rose*, and *The Cowboy's Rose* in L&L Dreamspell's Anthologies.
www.bettygordon.com

Bushwoman's Bannock

Ingredients:

3 cups flour
Pinch of salt
2 Tbsp bacon grease
1 tsp baking powder
Water
Seasonal berries

Combine all ingredients except berries and knead well into a stiff batter. Add berries gently and form into patties ½ inch thick. Heat in a cast-iron pan or seasoned griddle. If you cook this outdoors at a fire, the pan can be leaned toward the fire, baking the top first.

Lou Allison, author of the Belle Palmer series: *Memories Are Murder, Murder, eh? Northern Winters Are Murder, Black Flies Are Murder,* and *Bush Poodles Are Murder.*
www.louallin.com

Casey Breakfast Casserole

Ingredients:

1 can crescent rolls
1 dozen eggs, beaten
2 cups shredded cheddar cheese
1 pound cooked sausage (or ham, finely chopped)
Salt and pepper to taste

Put a fine layer of lard or shortening into a long 9" x 13" casserole dish, covering sides and bottom. Roll out crescent roll dough in the casserole, pressing into the corners. Crumble the meat over the dough. Pour eggs over meat. Sprinkle cheese over eggs. Bake 45 minutes to 1 hour at 350° F or until eggs are done and dough is brown. Cool before cutting into squares.

Kim Smith, author of The Shannon Wallace Mysteries: *Avenging Angel* and *Buried Angel*.
www.mkimsmith.com
www.writingspace.blogspot.com
www.blogtalkradio.com/kims
www.murderby4.blogspot.com

Clandestine Cheese Puffs

Ingredients:

8 oz package (2 cups) grated sharp cheddar cheese
1 cup plain flour
1 stick (1/2 cup) butter
¼ tsp salt (optional)

Using your hands, blend all ingredients together and form into a large ball. Refrigerate for at least one hour.

Preheat oven to 350° F. Roll into 1" balls and place on cookie sheet about an inch apart. Bake for approximately 15 minutes until bottom is browned. Top will be soft. Do not over bake.

Keith Donnelly, author of the Donald Youngblood Mystery series: *Three Deuces Down* and *Three Days Dead*.
www.donaldyoungbloodmysteries.com

Dazed Angel Biscuits

Ingredients:

2 packages (1/4 oz each) active dry yeast
¼ cup warm water (110-115° F)
2 cups warm buttermilk (110-115° F)
5 cups all-purpose flour
1/3 cup sugar
1 Tbsp baking powder
1 tsp salt
1 cup melted butter or margarine

Dissolve yeast in warm water. Let stand for 5 minutes. Stir in buttermilk and set aside. In large mixing bowl combine flour, sugar, baking powder, soda, and salt. Cut in butter until mixture resembles coarse meal. Stir in yeast mixture, mixing well. Turn dough out on lightly floured surface and knead 3-4 times. Roll to ½ inch thickness. Cut with a 2 ½ inch biscuit cutter. Place on lightly greased baking sheet. Cover and let rise in a warm place about 1 ½ hours. Bake at 450° F for 8-10 minutes. Lightly brush with melted butter. Yields about 2 ½ dozen.

H.L. Chandler, author of *The Keepers*.
www.hlchandler.bravehost.com

Deadly Sisters Blueberry Breakfast Bake

Ingredients:

8 slices white bread or wheat bread, cut into 1-inch pieces (about six cups)
1 8 oz package cream cheese, chilled and cut into 1/2 inch cubes
1 cup fresh blueberries
8 eggs
1 ½ cups milk (low fat or nonfat is okay)
1 cup blueberry syrup

Grease 11" x 7" baking dish. Spread half of the bread pieces evenly in baking dish. Top with cream cheese. Sprinkle with blueberries then spread remaining bread over the blueberries. Beat the eggs and milk in a medium bowl until blended; pour over bread. Cover unbaked mixture tightly with aluminum foil and refrigerate at least 8 hours, but not longer than 24 hours. When ready to bake, heat oven to 350° F. Bake covered for 30 minutes; uncover and bake 25-30 minutes longer or until top is puffed and center is set. Serve with blueberry syrup.
Courtesy of Amid Summer's Inn, Cedar City, Utah

Morgan St. James, author of *A Corpse in the Soup, Seven Deadly Samovars, Saying Goodbye to Miss Molly,* and *The World Outside The Window.*
www.silversistersmysteries.com
www.morganstjames-author.com

Flipped-Out Adirondack Flapjacks

4 eggs, separated
1 Tbsp sugar
¼ tsp salt
2 cups milk
2 Tbsp butter
2 cups flour
2 tsp baking powder

Butter or peanut oil for frying pancakes
Maple syrup, butter, whipped cream for topping

Beat egg whites until stiff.
In large bowl, beat egg yolks, then add remaining ingredients through baking powder, and mix until smooth. Mixture will be somewhat thin. Fold in egg whites. Heat butter or oil on griddle, fry flapjacks, turning once when bubbles cover surface of flapjack. Serve with melted butter, real maple syrup and top with whipped cream.
Used with permission from Mirror Lake Inn, Lake Placid, NY

Harol Marshall, author of *Holy Death* and *A Corpse for Cuamantla*.
www.harolmarshall.com

Killer Cornbread Recipe

Ingredients:

1 package Trader Joe's® Cornbread Mix

Add the following:

1 cup of oatmeal
¼ cup ground flaxseed
1 cup of 1% milk
½ cup dried cranberries or blueberries
1/3 cup raw almond slivers
1 tsp of ginger (for digestion)
1 tsp of cinnamon

In addition, the recipe on the package calls for one egg (large or extra large).
Use only a dash of olive oil or canola oil rather than the half cup suggested on the box. Mix just until moist.

Use a canola spray to grease 8" x 8" x 2" baking pan. Then pour evenly and bake at 350 degrees forty minutes until golden brown. For a nuttier flavor, remove at thirty minutes and place walnut bits on top.

Jacqueline Seewald, author of *The Drowning Pool* and *The Inferno Collection*.
www.jacquelineseewald.com

Malicious Mosquito Toast

Ingredients:

4 slices high fiber wheat bread cut in half (non diabetic may use white bread if desired)
1 egg
½ cup milk

Topping:
1 8 oz pkg cream cheese, softened
1 tsp milk
½ tsp vanilla
½ cup raisins
½ cup chopped pecans

Beat egg with milk in a bowl. Dip pieces of bread in the egg and milk mixture. Brown the pieces of bread in a pre-warmed skillet (similar to French toast). Mix the cream cheese with the milk and vanilla. Add the artificial sweetener until it achieves the level of sweetness desired.

Stir in the raisins and pecans.

Serve the topping on the side, allowing each person to spread the amount desired on the toast. The raisins are the simulation of mosquitoes on the toast. This is especially good served with Mimosas.

Loretta Wheeler, author of the story *Dark Pleasures* in an L&L Dreamspell anthology.
www.lorettawheeler.com

Murderous Sour Cream Muffins

Ingredients:

2 cups flour
¼ cup sugar
2 tsp baking powder
½ tsp baking soda
½ tsp salt
1 egg, beaten
1 cup sour cream
1/3 cup milk

¼ cup cooking oil

Preheat oven to 400° F.
Sift dry ingredients. Combine egg, sour cream, milk, and oil.
Make a well in the center of dry ingredients. Fill well-greased
muffin cups 2/3 full. Bake for 20 to 25 minutes.

Susanne Marie Knight, author of *Grave Future*.
www.susanneknight.com

Pinnacle Peak Fry Bread

Ingredients:

4 Tbsp honey
3 Tbsp lard (lard is the traditional shortening; vegetable oil may
be substituted)
1 Tbsp salt
2 cups hot water
1 package active dry yeast
3 cups unbleached white flour
2 tsp baking powder
2 to 4 cups additional flour

Prepare dough two hours before cooking.

Mix together honey, lard or vegetable oil, and salt. Stir in hot water and mix well. Sprinkle yeast on top of mixture. Cover with a cloth and allow to stand about ten minutes, until yeast bubbles. Add flour and baking powder. Stir well. Add more flour (2 to 4 cups) until dough is firm and cleans hands when mixed.

Place dough in greased bowl, turning over to grease top. Cover and allow to rise until dough doubles in bulk (about thirty minutes). Punch down and divide in half, then tear each half into eight parts (each ball of dough should be about the size of a peach).

Heat one inch or more of lard or vegetable oil to 375° F in a frying pan or deep fat fryer. Take a ball of dough and flatten with hands, using a stretching action until the dough is very thin and round (about six to eight inches in diameter). Poke a hole in the middle and drop dough into lard or oil. Fry until golden (turning once), about one-and-a-half minutes per side.

Remove from lard or vegetable oil. Drain on paper towels. Top with powdered or cinnamon sugar and honey or jam and serve immediately.

For a more substantial meal, top fried dough with favorite hamburger or taco fixings: shredded beef or chicken, shredded cheese, lettuce, tomato, onion, guacamole, taco sauce, salsa.

Twist Phelan, author of the Pinnacle Peak Mystery series: *Family Claims, Spurred Ambition, Heir Apparent, False Fortune.* www.twistphelan.com

Pumpin' Bread

Ingredients:

2 cups canned pumpkin
1 cup vegetable oil
2 ½ cups sugar
4 beaten eggs
3 ¼ cups flour
1 tsp baking powder
1 tsp baking soda
½ tsp clove powder
1 tsp nutmeg
2 tsp salt
1 tsp cinnamon

Mix all ingredients and pour into 2 greased bread pans. Bake 1 hour at 350° F.

Teresa Leigh Judd, author of *Quick on the Draw* in *Deadly Ink 2009* (Second Place Winner) and *Deja Vu* in *Romance of My Dreams.* www.lldreamspell.com

Raven's Apple Bread

Ingredients:

1 cup vegetable oil
3 eggs
2 cups sugar
1 tsp vanilla
4 cups apples, diced (I use Granny Smith)
3 cups flour
1 tsp cinnamon
1 tsp nutmeg
1 tsp baking soda
1 tsp baking powder
1 tsp salt

Mix oil, eggs, sugar, and vanilla in a bowl. In another bowl mix flour, cinnamon, nutmeg, baking soda, baking powder and salt. Add flour mixture to oil mixture and stir until well combined. Add the apples and stir until they're mixed well into the dough— there's a lot of apples in this, so don't worry if they're not all covered in dough even when you put it in the pan. Divide into two loaf pans and bake at 300° F for 1 to 1 ½ hours or until a toothpick inserted in center comes out clean.
Makes 2 loaves.

Raven Bower, author of *Apparitions.*
www.ravenbower.com

Sinister Scones

Ingredients:

2 cups (280 g) flour
2 tsp baking powder
1 Tbsp sugar
½ tsp salt
4 Tbsp butter
2 eggs, well beaten
1 cup (1 dL) cream
Optional ingredients:
Dried fruit
Chocolate chips
Nuts

Preheat the oven to 425° F (220° C). Lightly butter a cookie sheet. Mix the flour, baking powder, sugar, and salt in a large bowl. If you want to add dried cherries, apples, raisins, walnuts, almonds, chocolate chips and the like, this is a good place to do it. I don't measure those ingredients, just mix in until I feel like there'll be a little of each in the individual scones.

Work in the butter with your fingers or a pastry blender. I generally cut the butter into thin slivers before adding. Work it until the mixture resembles coarse meal. Add the eggs and cream and stir until blended.

Turn dough out onto a lightly floured board and knead for about a minute. Pat or roll the dough until it's about ½ inch thick and roughly circular in shape. Cut into wedges. Makes about a dozen scones. Place on cookie sheet and bake about 15 minutes. Turn the cookie sheet about halfway through to assure even browning. Tops should have a nice golden look when done.

Mike Nettleton—Co author, *The Big Grabowski.*
www.krillbooks.com

Stirred-Up Apple Raisin Bread

Ingredients:

2 cups flour
2 tsp baking powder
½ tsp baking soda
½ tsp salt
¾ cup sugar or Splenda
1 cup milk
2 eggs
1 Tbsp Canola oil
2 tsp vanilla
2 medium apples, peeled and shredded
¼ cup raisins

Mix dry ingredients together, set aside. Mix liquid ingredients then combine with dry ingredients. Stir in apples and raisins. Pour into loaf pan sprayed with non-stick cooking spray. Bake at 350° F for 45 to 55 minutes until cake tester inserted in center comes out clean.

Caitlyn Hunter, author of *The Secret Life of Alice Smitty*, in an L&L Dreamspell anthology.
http://caitlynhunter.com

Riveting Garlic Bread

Ingredients:

French Bread (long loaf, uncut)
Spreadable butter
Parmesan Cheese
Mozzarella Cheese, shredded
Mrs. Dash Garlic and Herb Seasoning

Cut loaf long-ways into two pieces.

Spread each cut side (not the crust) with butter.
Sprinkle parmesan cheese and mozzarella cheese over it.
Cover that with the seasoning mix and bake at 350° F until cheese
is melted.

Kim Smith, author of the Shannon Wallace Mystery series: *Avenging Angel* and *Buried Angel.*
www.mkimsmith.com
www.writingspace.blogspot.com
www.murderby4.blogspot.com
www.blogtalkradio.com/kims

Tortured Tortillas and Eggs

Ingredients:

4 eggs
6 corn tortillas
Fresh cilantro
1½ cups of your favorite salsa (preferably chunky)

In a bowl, beat the four eggs and set aside.
Cut tortillas into one inch by three inch strips.
Chop cilantro and set aside.

Pour a generous amount of canola or other oil in a medium, ten inch pan. Set heat to medium. When the oil is hot place half of the tortilla strips into the pan and cook until they are crisp. Remove strips and place them on paper towels. Place the rest of the strips into the pan and cook until they are crisp, then place on paper towels.

Drain most of the oil from the pan and set heat to medium high. Place all of the crisp tortilla strips back into the pan and immediately pour the beaten eggs over the strips. Working very quickly, stir the mixture until the eggs are fully cooked, coating most of the strips which should remain as crisp as possible. Immediately pour the salsa over the entire mixture, but do not stir, then remove the pan from the stove. Sprinkle with chopped cilantro and serve with refried beans on the side.

Ernesto (Ernie) Patino, author of *Web of Secrets*.
www.ernestopatino.com

Wacky Zucchini Bread

Ingredients:

1 ½ cups sugar
3 eggs
1 cup vegetable oil
3 tsp vanilla
2 ½ cups zucchini, unpeeled, chopped
3 cups self-rising flour
3 ½ tsp ground cinnamon
1 small can (20 oz) crushed pineapple, undrained

Preheat oven to 350° F.
Cream eggs, oil, and sugar together.
Add zucchini and vanilla.
Add rest of ingredients.
Grease and flour 2 loaf pans.
Bake 45 minutes to 1 hour (until inserted toothpick comes out clean).

Christy Tillery French, award-winning author of *The Bodyguard and the Snitch* and *Chasing Secrets*.
http://christytilleryfrench.com
http://damesofdialogue.wordpress.com

WACKY
ZUCCHINI BREAD

Criminal Bites, Dips, and Beverages

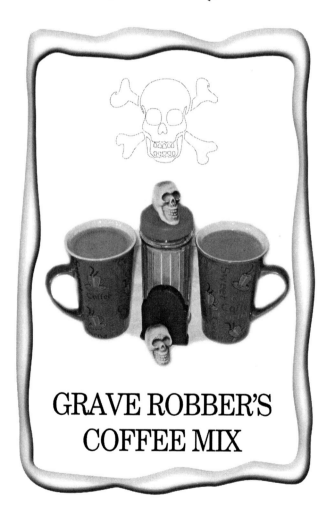

GRAVE ROBBER'S COFFEE MIX

Bloody Marys

Ingredients:

2 jiggers vodka
¼ tsp salt
1 ½ cups tomato juice
1/8 tsp pepper
¼ cup lemon juice
2 dashes Tabasco sauce
¼ tsp Worcestershire sauce

Put ingredients into a blender and cover. Process at Frappe a few seconds until frothy. Strain into small highball glasses.

H.L. Chandler, author of *The Keepers.*
www.hlchandler.bravehost.com

Cocky Franks

Ingredients:

1 cup barbecue sauce (your choice)
1 package plain cocktail franks

In medium saucepan, bring the barbecue sauce to a boil. Add the franks and return to a boil. Reduce heat and simmer for 15 minutes.

Stacy Juba, author of *Twenty-Five Years Ago Today, Sink or Swim,* and *Face-Off.*
www.stacyjuba.com

Coffin-oozing Brie (Baked Brie)

Lace Baskets
Ingredients:

1 four inch round Brie Cheese or a wedge of a larger Brie
1 sheet Pepperidge Farm Puff Pastry, room temperature (package of 2 sheets can be found in the frozen food section of your market)
¼ cup packed brown sugar (enough to generously cover the top of the cheese)
1 egg
½ cup walnut or pecan pieces*

Lay puff pastry sheet out on a cookie sheet sprayed with PAM. Remove paper and wrapping from cheese. Lay the cheese on the center of the puff pastry (Note: leave the rind on because it's edible and adds to the flavor.) Press the brown sugar over the top of the cheese. Lay the nuts on top of the brown sugar. Wrap the cheese in the pastry dough like a package. Seal the edges of the pastry dough tightly, completely enclosing the cheese. Beat the egg until frothy and then brush the egg over the top of the crust.

Poke about four air holes in the top of the pastry so steam can escape. Bake at 400° F for 20 minutes, until golden. Turn the temperature of the oven down to 325° F and bake another 20 to 25 minutes. Remove from oven and cool slightly. Remove from baking sheet to serving plate, surround with crackers and/or fruit.

*Try substituting slices of green apple or pears for the walnuts.

Gayle Wigglesworth, author of The Claire Gulliver Mysteries, Mud to Ashes, a Pottery Mystery, and Gayle's Legacy: Recipes, Hints and Stories Culled from a Lifelong Relationship with Food. www.gaylewigglesworth.com
www.facebook.com/gaylewigglesworth

Cold Shot Brandy Alexander

Ingredients:

1 finger shot glass quality Brandy
½ of pint carton chocolate ice cream

Blend until smooth and fairly thick. Serve as summer drink or dessert.

Susan Whitfield, author of the award-winning Logan Hunter Mystery series: *Genesis Beach, Just North of Luck, Hell Swamp,* and *Sin Creek.*
www.susanwhitfieldonline.com
www.susanwhitfield.blogspot.com

Creamed Cheese Dip

Ingredients:

2 - 8 oz packages cream cheese (softened to room temp)
1 - 8 oz can crushed pineapple (drained)
2 Tbsp finely chopped onion
½ cup finely chopped pecans
½ cup finely chopped green pepper

Stir all ingredients together in a bowl. Refrigerate at least 3 hours to allow the flavors to blend. May be formed into a ball and rolled in additional chopped pecans or served at room temperature as a dip.

Caitlyn Hunter, author of *The Secret Life of Alice Smitty* an L&L Dreamspell anthology.
www.caitlynhunter.com

Deadly-icious Cracker Spread

Ingredients:

¼ cup real mayonnaise
¼ cup sour cream
¼ cup cream cheese

3 Tbsp freshly chopped chives (3 tsp if using dried herbs)
Can also be made with dill, basil or cilantro

Mix your choice of herb (or a combination of 2 herbs) with mayo, sour cream and cream cheese. Serve in a bowl to accompany a variety of crackers or spread on thin slices of baguette and toast lightly under the broiler to serve warm.

Suzanne Young, author of *Murder by Yew*.
www.suzanneyoungbooks.com

Easy Prey Rollups

Ingredients:

1 whole wheat tortilla (8 inch)
2 Tbsp 1/3 less fat cream cheese
2 Tbsp canned crushed pineapple, drained
2 Tbsp chopped walnuts
1 lettuce leaf
6 slices thinly sliced brown sugar ham

Spread cream cheese over tortilla, top with remaining ingredients in layers. Roll up tortilla and cut into bite size pieces.

Kim Smith, author of The Shannon Wallace Mysteries: *Avenging Angel* and *Buried Angel*.
http://www.mkimsmith.com
http://www.pubd2b.wordpress.com
http://www.writingspace.blogspot.com
http://www.murderby4.blogspot.com
http://www.blogtalkradio.com/kims

Fiendish Fiesta Dip

Ingredients:

2 - 11 oz cans Mexican corn, undrained
8 oz sour cream
8 oz Kraft Mayo –not Miracle Whip
1 - 4 oz can green chiles
2 cups shredded cheese
1 bunch green onions, chopped
2 jalapeno peppers, chopped

Mix all ingredients and refrigerate 8 hrs.

Anne Patrick, author of 'Sweet' Edge of Your Seat Suspense: *Every Skull Tells A Story, Journey to Redemption, Lethal Dreams, Dark Alliance, Ties That Bind, Out of the Darkness*, and *Fire And Ash*. www.suspensebyanne.blogspot.com

Grave-Robber's Coffee Mix

Ingredients:

1/3 cup instant coffee
1/3 cup creamer
1/3 cup sugar (or sweetener to taste)
¼ cup cocoa

Mix well and store in tightly covered container. Use 2 tablespoons of mix per 8 ozcup and add very hot water.

Marilyn Gardiner, author of the Winsom series: *Dancing Ladies, Window On Windemere, Banjo Eyes*, and *Mistletoe and Holly*. http://marilyn-gardiner.com

Killer Doll Dip

Ingredients:

1 large box Velveeta Processed Cheese, cut into 1inch cubes
2 cans pre-made chili
1 jar salsa
Tortillas or cut raw vegetables

In large microwavable bowl put cubed Velveeta. Add chili. Add salsa. Microwave on full power and stir periodically. Once blended, it is ready to serve.

Angelica Hart and Zi, author of *Killer Dolls, Snake Dance,* and *Chasing Gravitas.*
www.angelicahartandzi.com

Lethal Three-Layer Fiesta Dip

Ingredients:

Bottom layer:
Large can of refried beans, small can of diced green chilies, salt to taste.
Blend the ingredients together in a bowl, then spread with a spatula on a party platter. Rinse the bowl with hot water and reuse for next layer.

Middle layer:
Pint of low-fat sour cream and half a package of taco seasoning.
Whip the two ingredients together in a bowl. Drop spoonfuls of the seasoned sour cream all over the bean layer and gently spread it, leaving an edge of the bean layer showing. Rinse the bowl with hot water to reuse for next layer.

Top layer:
Guacamole (use store bought guacamole, your own recipe, or make an easy version by blending two avocados with three tablespoons of your favorite salsa.)

Drop the guacamole by spoonfuls and gently spread it, leaving an edge of the sour cream layer showing.

Garnish the top with colorful additions: finely diced black olives, finely diced red onion, and grated sharp cheddar cheese.

L.J. Sellers, author of *The Sex Club* and *Secrets to Die For.*
www.ljsellers.com

Mad Russian Tea

Ingredients:

5 cups boiling water
5 tea bags
2 cinnamon sticks
5 cloves—embedding them in a piece of orange rind makes them easy to remove after steeping
1 quart pineapple juice
1 quart orange juice
1 cup lemon juice, fresh is best
Sugar, honey or sweetener to taste

Add boiling water to tea and spices then steep for about 20 minutes. Mix all juices with tea in large pitcher. Steep again for another 10 minutes. Serve hot or cold.

Joyce and Jim Lavene, authors of *Ghastly Glass* and other mysteries.
www.joyceandjimlavene.com

Meat Cleaver's Taco Dip

Ingredients:

1 large carton sour cream
1 large pkg cream cheese
1 pkg taco seasoning
Chopped tomatoes, onion, lettuce, green peppers, olives, cheddar cheese

Beat cream cheese until smooth. Add sour cream and taco seasoning, blending well. Spread in a 9" x 13" size pan (non-metal). Top with chopped vegetables. Serve with nacho chips.

Miss Mae, author of *Said the Spider to the Fly, When the Bough Breaks* and *It's Elementary, My Dear Winifred.*
www.missmaesite.com

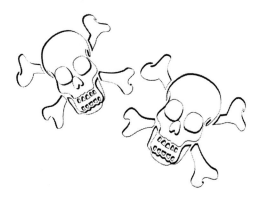

Mushrooms to Die For

Ingredients:

1 dozen medium mushrooms
3 Tbsp finely chopped red onion
¼ cup finely chopped fresh spinach
½ cup seasoned Italian breadcrumbs
3 Tbsp grated Parmesan cheese
Fresh pepper
Salt
Olive oil

Clean mushrooms with a paper towel. (Do not wash!) Cut off and toss the pithy part of the stems and pop out the remainder with a spoon, leaving a nice hollowed out area to stuff.
Mince the portion you popped out and place in a bowl.
Mix in onion, spinach, cheese, and breadcrumbs. Grind in a little pepper. Salt is optional, add it to taste.
Add just enough olive oil so the mixture barely holds together if you squeeze it in your hand.
Pack the mixture into the mushroom caps so it's domed up. (The domes will shrink as the mushrooms bake.)

Place mushrooms on an oiled pan and bake at 350° F for about 15 minutes (more or less depending on the size of the mushrooms and the heat of your oven) until mushrooms are soft and the top of the stuffing is browned and a little crisp.

Serve immediately as appetizers or as a side dish with steak, fish, or pasta.

Carolyn J. Rose, author of *Hemlock Lake* and co-author of *The Big Grabowski*.
www.deadlyduomysteries.com

Nutty Brie

Ingredients:

¼ cup brown sugar
¼ cup pecans
1 Tbsp Brandy
1 - 4 oz Round Brie

Stir together sugar, nuts, and brandy. Cover and chill for 24 hrs. Preheat oven to 500° F. Cut Brie in half and place on pie plate. Heat until Brie oozes. Spread mixture over Brie until sugar melts. Serve with fresh fruit and crackers.

Susan Whitfield, author of the award-winning Logan Hunter Mystery series: *Genesis Beach, Just North of Luck, Hell Swamp,* and *Gator Creek.*
www.susanwhitfieldonline.com
www.susanwhitfield.blogspot.com

Ogeechee Pecan Bites

Pecan orchards figure into Linda's books. The town, Ogeechee, is in pecan country.

For the base/crust:
1 cup butter
½ cup powdered sugar
2 cups flour

Melt the butter and combine it with the sugar and flour. Press into a 9" x 13" baking pan. Bake about 15 minutes at 350° F.

For the topping/filling:
1 cup chopped pecans
2 eggs
1 ½ cups brown sugar
2 Tbsp melted butter
Dash of salt
¼ tsp vanilla

Mix the topping ingredients together and pour over the baked base. Bake about 15 minutes at 350° F. When cool, cut into bite-sized pieces.

Linda Berry, author of The Trudy Roundtree Mysteries.
www.ogeechee.avigne.org

Ogre's Roll-ups

Ingredients:

Sliced sandwich ham
Cream cheese, softened
Pickled okra (in the pickle section of your store)

Pat the ham slices dry and spread with cream cheese. Cut the stem off two pieces of okra and lay the pieces across the narrow end of the ham, with the stem ends at the outside edge and the pointy ends crossing in the middle. (You can eat the stems while you finish the roll-up.) Roll like a jellyroll. Chill before slicing. Each roll makes six little flowers about ¾" to 1 or 2" wide. Even people who think they don't like okra like these.

Linda Berry, author of The Trudy Roundtree Mysteries.
www.ogeechee.avigne.org

Ornery Nut Spread

Ingredients:

6 oz cream cheese or Neuchâtel cheese
½ cup mayo (I like Miracle Whip)
½ cup chopped pecans
1 cup chopped green olives with pimento
Dash of black pepper

Combine everything and store tightly covered in refrigerator. Serve as a dip with Ritz crackers, or as a spread on small rye rounds of bread.

Marilyn Gardiner, author of the Winsom series: *Dancing Ladies, Window On Windemere, Banjo Eyes, and Mistletoe and Holly.* http://marilyn-gardiner.com

Pizza Witches

Ingredients:

1 lb hamburger, cooked, drained and cooled
1 pkg shredded mozzarella cheese
1 pkg shredded cheddar cheese
1 can tomato sauce or pizza sauce
½ to 1 tsp Oregano
Add garlic salt, salt, and pepper to taste

Mix all ingredients and refrigerate.

When ready to serve:
Spread additional pizza sauce on sliced Italian Bread or small wraps (extra pizza sauce is optional).
Spread pizza mixture on top of sauce.
Broil for 2 to 5 minutes or until bread is toasted.

For more fun, add your favorite toppings like pepperoni or green olives stuffed with jalapenos.

Denise Robbins, author of It *Happens in Threes, Killer Bunny Hill, and Connect the Dots.*
http://deniserobbins.com

Reckless Sailor's Key Lime Dip

Ingredients:

6 fresh key limes or ½ cup key lime juice
1 16 oz can sweetened condensed milk
1 package vanilla wafers
Ice

Squeeze six fresh key limes for ½ cup fresh juice. Add a little zest from the skin if you wish. Stir with whip into one small can sweetened, condensed milk (may use non-fat variety—condensed is the secret). Let set a few minutes while opening a package of vanilla wafers. If you are not on a sailboat and/or have ice, whip up a dollop or two of whipped cream. Also, cool the key lime mixture on the ice or in a fridge; the longer it cools, the better set. Serve as a dip with the vanilla wafers or any tea biscuit or lay wafers close together in 8-inch pie dish and spread mixture over the top.

D.K. Christi, author of *Ghost Orchid, The Bamboo Connection, The Ice Storm, The View From The Balcony, Maddie's Christmas Spider Lily, My Viet Nam Vet, A Walk on the Beach, The Magic Box, What Happens in Jamaica Stays in Jamaica, Affairs of the Heart—The Rulebook, Chalk,* and more.
www.dkchristi.com

Ruptured Dates

Ingredients:

12 fresh dates
½ block cream cheese, softened

Whip cheese until fluffy. Slice dates open and remove pits. Spoon approximately 2 tsp of cheese into date.

Variations: Try Honey-Pecan soft cream cheese. You can also add honey and cinnamon while whipping if desired.

T.L. Ryder, author of *No Place Like Home (Under The Moon Anthology)*.
www.underthemoon.org/undeadembrace.html

Stuffed-In-The-Trunk Mushrooms

Ingredients:

1 lb fresh jumbo mushrooms
1 chopped onion
¼ cup olive oil
6 crumbled saltine crackers
½ cup bread crumbs
¼ cup parmesan cheese
1 Tbsp chopped walnuts
1/2 cup Red wine
Pinch of basil
Pinch of thyme
Salt
Pepper

Clean mushrooms with paper towel. Remove stems, set caps aside. Chop stems and combine with chopped onion. Sauté in olive oil until tender. Remove from heat. Add saltine crackers, bread crumbs, parmesan cheese, pinch of basil and thyme. Add chopped walnuts and mix well. Salt and pepper to taste.

Pour wine in shallow baking pan. Carefully stuff mushroom caps (trunks) with crumb mixture. Arrange in pan with wine, cap side down, stuffed side up. Bake in 300-degree oven until tender (depends how many in pan). Do not overcook. Serves 4 to 6.

When served, crumbly mixture should be kind of crunchy or dry to hold everything together so you can pick them up to eat, if you choose. If overcooked, or if too much wine is used, mushrooms and everything may be soggy.

Mary Deal, author of *River Bones*.
www.WriteAnyGenre.com

Tainted Tea Mix

Ingredients:

2 cups instant orange drink mix
½ cup strawberry lemonade mix
1 cup diet lemon iced tea mix
1 tsp cinnamon

Pour ingredients into bowl and stir. Store in tightly covered container. To serve, place 1 tablespoon of mixture into cup, fill with 6 ounces of boiling water, and enjoy! Serves approximately 56.

Susanne Marie Knight, author of *Tainted Tea For Two*.
www.susanneknight.com

Twisted Pimiento Cheese

Ingredients:

1 cup Sharp cheddar cheese, coarsely shredded
¾ cup pimientos, drained and smashed with a fork
Peppercorns, subjected to blunt force trauma
Mayonnaise, only enough to hold it together

Spread on rye bread (option to torture in panini press).
Serve with chopped fruit and nuts or serve on greens and top with a mountain of tortilla chips.

Maggie Bishop, Cozy author of *Perfect For Framing*.
http://maggiebishop1.tripod.com
http://damesofdialogue.wordpress.com
http://authorasguestspeaker.110mb.com

MUSHROOMS
TO DIE FOR

Devilish Desserts

CRAZY PUMPKIN CRISP

Ba's* Pound Cake

Ingredients:

2 sticks butter
1 2/3 cups sugar
2 cups flour
5 eggs
1 Tbsp vanilla

Cream butter and sugar thoroughly (by hand or with an electric mixer). Add eggs, one at a time, beating well after each one. Add flour and vanilla and mix thoroughly. Put batter in well-greased tube pan. Put in cold oven, turn oven to 350° F and bake one hour. Note—this is not a high-rising cake—it's dense and delicious. For a decadent treat, cut a slice, butter it, and run it under the broiler.

* Ba is Vicki's grandmother.

Vicki Lane, author of the Elizabeth Goodweather Mystery series: *In A Dark Season, Old Wounds, Art's Blood, and Signs in the Blood.* www.vickilanemysteries.com

Boozed-up Figgy Pudding

Dickens places it on Bob Cratchit's table in his famous story, *A Christmas Carol*, and my real life character, 18th century Mary Wollstonecraft, enjoyed it on many a holiday.

12 oz dried figs, de-stemmed, simmered and cooled
5 slices white bread
1 stick butter
1 cup chopped pecans
3 eggs
1 cup sugar
¼ cup molasses
½ cup cream sherry
1 tsp cinnamon
¼ tsp salt

Chop the figs finely. Toast the bread lightly and break into small pieces. Set figs and bread aside. Cream the butter and sugar in a double boiler. Add eggs and beat 3 minutes until light and fluffy. Mix the molasses, sherry, cinnamon, and salt, and then blend in the figs, bread, and pecans with a spoon.

Butter and sugar the mold, then pour the mix into the mold. Place a trivet in the bottom of a wide, deep pan; fill it half way up the mold with water and bring to a boil. Seal the mold with aluminum foil, and cover the pan as well. Run at a slow boil for 3 hours, checking the water occasionally. (Keep a kettle of hot water handy to add without slowing down steaming.)
After 3 hours of steaming, remove the mold from the kettle. Uncover and place a plate upside down on the open mold, and turn the plate over to release the pudding. Serve warm.
Can be made ahead, wrapped in foil, and refrigerated. To reheat, either steam again or use a microwave oven.

Foamy Sauce (for Figgy Pudding):

1/3 cup butter
1 egg
1 ½ cups confectioner's sugar
1 tsp vanilla extract
2 Tbsp rum
1 cup whipping cream (add a little extra rum before whipping)

Beat the egg and the butter. Add sugar, vanilla, and rum, and mix well. Fold in the whipping cream.
Can be made an hour or two ahead. Chill until ready to serve.

Nancy Means Wright, award-winning author of the Northern Spy series, the Ruth Willmarth series, and the Mary Wollstonecraft series.
www.nancymeanswright.com

Brittle Bones

Make on a cold, clear day/night*

Ingredients:

¼ cup water
½ cup light Karo syrup
1 cup granulated sugar
2 cups raw peanuts, shelled
1 tsp baking soda

Note: Before you begin, fill sink half full of hot soapy water, prepare greased cookie sheet and place measured soda on a napkin. This moves fast! No time to wander off.

In a black cast-iron skillet, boil water, syrup, and sugar. Add nuts and cook until about 6 to 8 nuts make a popping sound. Immediately remove from heat and add soda. Stir well and quickly pour onto greased pan. Toss skillet into suds for easy cleanup. Take cookie sheet outside and leave for 15 minutes before checking for brittleness. (I often use my freezer since it's outside. A deck rail is fine if the wind isn't blowing.)
* If the air is damp, brittle will be sticky.

Once brittle has set, snap into small pieces and enjoy.

Susan Whitfield, author of the award-winning Logan Hunter Mystery series: *Genesis Beach, Just North of Luck, Hell Swamp, and Sin Creek.*
www.susanwhitfieldonline.com
www.suanwhitfield.blogspot.com

Clobbered Peach Cobbler

Put oven at 350° F and while it is heating, put 1 stick butter in 9" x 12" pan inside oven, and heat until bubbling, but not brown.

Mix together:

1 cup self-rising flour
1 cup sugar
2/3 cup milk
A small pinch salt
1 tsp of lemon juice
1 tsp of vanilla

Once that is mixed, take the pan of bubbling butter out of the oven and pour the mix into the pan immediately. The butter should come up over the flour to make the very yummy crust.

Use drained sliced peaches. If frozen let thaw a little so the juice is not watery. Canned and bottled work as well, and fresh are the best. Place peaches across the pan.

Bake for about 45 minutes to an hour so that the dough is done and golden all around. Top with whipped cream, ice cream, or whatever suits your fancy.
May substitute other fruits.

Iona McAvoy, author of *Jadead* in an L&L Dreamspell anthology.
www.ionamcavoy.com

Cracked Coconut Pie

Ingredients:

1 stick butter or margarine, melted
2 cups sugar
5 eggs, beaten
1 tsp lemon flavoring
1 tsp vanilla flavoring
½ tsp salt
¾ cup buttermilk
1 ¾ cups angel flaked coconut

Cream together butter and sugar. Add beaten eggs a little at a time and stir. Stir in flavoring, salt and buttermilk. Fold in coconut. Pour into 2 unbaked pie shells and bake at 325° F for approximately 45 minutes. Should be lightly brown and firm. Serves 6 to 8.

Lynette Hall Hampton, author of *Stetson Mold* and the Reverend Willa Hinshaw series.
www.lynettehallhampton.com

Crazy Pumpkin Crisp

Ingredients:

1 - 15 ounce can pumpkin (not pie filling)
1 cup evaporated milk
1 cup sugar
1 tsp vanilla
½ tsp cinnamon
1 box butter recipe cake mix
1 cup chopped pecans
1 cup melted butter

Preheat oven to 350° F.
Mix pumpkin, milk, sugar, vanilla, and cinnamon together and pour into greased 9" x13" pan.
Sprinkle cake mix evenly over top.
Sprinkle on pecans.
Pour butter evenly over top.

Bake at 350° F for one hour.

Christy Tillery French, award-winning author of *The Bodyguard and the Snitch* and *Chasing Secrets*.
http://christytilleryfrench.com
http://damesofdialogue.wordpress.com

Crushed Pineapple Torte

Crust:

30 vanilla wafers
1/3 stick softened butter
1/8 cup sugar

Crush vanilla wafers until fine. Add 1/3 stick of softened butter and 1/8 cup of sugar. Mix with hands. Save some mixture for top. Press mixture into torte pan. Bake at 375° F for 5 minutes. Let crust cool.

Filling:

24 large marshmallows
13 oz can crushed pineapple
½ pint whipping cream, whipped

Drain juice from pineapple and add to marshmallows in a double boiler and heat until marshmallows dissolve. When mixture cools, add pineapple and whipped cream.

Pour filling into prepared crust and top with remaining crumb mixture.

Jodi Diderrich, author of *Hiram's Rock* in an L&L Dreamspell anthology.
www.jodididerrich.com

Cutthroat Chocolate Pie

Ingredients:

3/4 cup sugar
2 rounded Tbsp unsweetened cocoa powder
3 rounded Tbsp flour
¼ tsp salt
1 cup evaporated milk
1 cup water
3 egg yolks
3 Tbsp butter
1 Tbsp vanilla

Combine dry ingredients in medium saucepan. Mix evaporated milk and water together in a small bowl or measuring cup. Pour just enough of this mixture into dry ingredients to make a thick paste.

Stir in egg yolks and mix very well. (This keeps the egg yolks from curdling when cooked.) Slowly stir in the rest of the milk/water mixture.

Cook over medium heat, stirring frequently until it boils and gets thick. Remove from heat.

Stir in butter and vanilla. After butter melts, pour into prepared, baked pie crust. Top with your favorite meringue (using whites from separated yolks) or whipped cream. Cool.

Sylvia Dickey Smith, author of *Dance On His Grave and Deadly Sins-Deadly Secrets.*
www.sylviadickeysmithbooks.wordpress.com
www.sylviadickeysmith.blogspot.com
www.lldreamspell.com

Deadly Chocolate Pudding Cake

Ingredients:

1 cup all purpose flour
¾ cup granulated sugar
1 cup brown sugar, packed
¼ cup + 2 Tbsp unsweetened cocoa
2 tsp baking powder
¼ tsp salt
2 Tbsp vegetable oil
½ cup milk
1 tsp vanilla
1¾ cups very hot water
Ice cream

Heat oven to 350° F. In an ungreased 9" x 9" x 2" baking pan mix flour, baking powder, salt, and 2 Tbsp cocoa. Add milk, vegetable oil and vanilla and stir well. Spread evenly over pan. Mix the brown sugar and ¼ cup cocoa together and sprinkle over the batter. Pour very hot water on top. Bake for about 40 minutes. Cool about 15 or 20 minutes. Spoon over dishes of ice cream and serve.

Notes: When you put this together don't worry about the hot water floating on top of the batter. You didn't do anything wrong. Trust me, it will be wonderful.

Try adding nuts with the brown sugar and cocoa you sprinkle over the top of the batter, before pouring the hot water on.

Gayle Wigglesworth, author of The Claire Gulliver Mysteries: *Tea is for Terror, Washington Weirdos, Intrigue in Italics, Cruisin' for a Bruisin', Malice in Mexico and Mud to Ashes*, a Pottery Mystery, and *Gayle's Legacy*: Recipes, Hints and Stories Culled from a Lifelong Relationship with Food.
www.gaylewigglesworth.com
www.facebook.com/gaylewigglesworth

Decadent Applesauce Cake

Ingredients:

1½ cups dark brown sugar
¾ cup oil
1½ cups applesauce with ½ tsp baking soda stirred in
2 cups flour
1 tsp cinnamon
1 tsp allspice
1 tsp soda
½ tsp salt
Raisins and chopped walnuts

Combine brown sugar and oil in bowl, mixing well. Add applesauce with soda. Then add flour and spices, other soda and salt. Mix well. Stir in raisins and nuts.
Pour into greased and floured 9" x 13" baking dish and bake at 350° F for 45-50 minutes or until toothpick comes out dry.

Kathleen Delaney, author of *Dying For A Change, Give First Place To Murder, and Murder For Dessert.*
www.kathleendelaney.net

Evil Chocoholic's Pie

Ingredients:

2 deep dish pie shells
8 oz unsweetened chocolate
4 sticks butter
8 eggs and 2 yolks (may substitute Egg Beaters)
1 cup heavy cream
5 cups sugar
1 Tbsp vanilla

Melt chocolate with butter. Fold eggs into cream and pour into chocolate mixture. Then add sugar gradually. Pour into shells and bake at 350° F for 40 minutes or until tops are fairly firm but center is still moist.

Susan Whitfield, author of the award-winning Logan Hunter Mystery series: *Genesis Beach, Just North of Luck, Hell Swamp, and Sin Creek.*
www.susanwhitfieldonline.com
www.susanwhitfield.blogspot.com

Fanatic's Fruitcake Cookies

Ingredients:

1 ½ cups raisins
¼ cup bourbon or brandy
3 cups flour
1 Tbsp baking soda
1 Tbsp cinnamon
1 tsp nutmeg
1 tsp ground cloves
½ cup butter
1 cup brown sugar
4 eggs
1 lb fruitcake mix (small candied cherries, citron, pineapple chunks)
2 cups pecans or walnuts
½ lb whole candied cherries for tops

Mix raisins and liquor. Let stand 1 hour while butter softens. Mix flour, soda, and 3 spices. In separate bowl, cream butter, add sugar, then eggs and beat until light and fluffy. Add flour mixture and mix until smooth. Add raisins, fruitcake mix, and nuts and mix well. Cover and chill overnight. With an ice cream scoop, shape into 1" balls, put on greased cookie sheets, and press a candied cherry into the top of each cookie. Bake at 325° F for 12-14 minutes. Makes about 6 dozen. When storing, separate with waxed paper because they'll stick to each other.

Beth Groundwater, author of *A Real Basket Case* and *To Hell in a Handbasket*.
www.bethgroundwater.com

Ghostly Gooseberry Pie

Ingredients:

1 quart fresh gooseberries, rounded measure
1/4 cup water
1 1/2 cups sugar
1/8 tsp salt
2 Tbsp tapioca (use 3 Tbsp for thicker pie)
1 tsp vinegar
Crust for double crust pie

Cook 1 cup gooseberries with 1/4 cup water, sugar, salt and tapioca. Cook until done and mash berries. Add remaining raw berries to the mashed ones and add vinegar. Pour into crust and cover with top crust. Bake at 400° F for about 40 minutes until browned and bubbly. Serves 8.

H. L. Chandler author of *The Keepers.*
www.hlchandler.bravehost.com

Guillotine Tuiles

Wright's character, Mary Wollstonecraft, (mother of Mary Shelley of Frankenstein fame) and a lover of almonds, discovered the classic French almond cookie, tuile, shaped like the curved tile one finds on terra cotta roofs. Here is one version of a tuile.

Ingredients:

2 egg whites
6 Tbsp soft butter or olive oil
½ cup of sugar
1 cup sliced almonds
½ cup of sifted flour
Dash of salt

Cream the sugar and butter together until fully blended, and then stir in the flour, egg whites, nuts, and salt. Grease a heavy cookie sheet, and drop the batter by teaspoons ½ inch apart, leaving room for the butter to spread. Bake in a 400° F oven for ten minutes or so, or until yellowish in the center and golden-brown on the edges. With a spatula, remove the tuiles and press them, one by one, while hot, onto a rolling pin. After two or three minutes, place them on a rack to cool. The recipe should make about two dozen tuiles.

Nancy Means Wright, award-winning author of the Northern Spy series, the Ruth Willmarth series, and the Mary Wollstonecraft series.
www.nancymeanswright.com

Howling Hot Apple Crisp

Ingredients:

7 Granny Smith apples, peeled and sliced
½ cup white rice flour
½ cup sugar
1 tsp ground cinnamon
½ tsp salt
1 stick butter, softened
Vanilla ice cream

Preheat oven to 350° F.

Place sliced apples in baking pan. In a bowl, blend together flour, sugar, cinnamon, salt, and butter. Spread the mixture over apples. Bake for about 30 minutes or until golden brown. Serve over a scoop of vanilla ice cream.

Michelle Hollstein-Matkins, author of the Aggie Underhill Mystery series.
www.MichelleAnnHollstein.com

Killer Cookies

Ingredients:

1 cup margarine or butter (2 cubes) melted and cooled slightly
1 cup brown sugar (packed)
1 cup granulated sugar
2 eggs (if you're using jumbo eggs reduce the water by half)
1 tsp vanilla
1 Tbsp of warm water (or ½ Tbsp if using jumbo eggs)
1 tsp of salt
1 tsp of baking soda
1 ½ cups flour
3 cups uncooked oatmeal
1 cup small M & Ms
1 cup peanut butter chips
1 cup dried blueberries (you could substitute cranberries, cherries or raisins)
1 cup peanuts

Heat oven to 350° F and spray two baking sheets with PAM. Mix butter and sugars until smooth. Beat the eggs in a small bowl and add to butter mixture, mixing well.

Put the water in a small bowl and add baking soda and salt to it. Stir until the soda and salt are dissolved, then add it to the batter and mix in well. Slowly add the flour, mixing it well as you go. Add the oatmeal, one cup at a time until the batter is completely mixed.

Stir in last four ingredients and let rest for 15 minutes. Drop generous teaspoons of dough onto the baking sheet about 1 inch apart. Bake until golden brown (approximately 12 to 15 minutes). Remove and let cool for five minutes before placing on a rack or paper towels to completely cool. Store in airtight containers. Note: This is a double recipe. These cookies do freeze very well.

Gayle Wigglesworth, author of the Claire Gulliver Mysteries: *Tea is for Terror, Washington Weirdos, Intrigue in Italics, Cruisin' for a Bruisin', and Malice in Mexico, and Mud to Ashes,* a Pottery Mystery, and *Gayle's Legacy*: Recipes, Hints and Stories Culled from a Lifelong Relationship with Food.
www.gaylewigglesworth.com
www.facebook.com/gaylewigglesworth

Lethal Fudge (no bake)

Ingredients:

1 – 1 gallon Ziploc bag (the kind that you have to press to seal)
1 pound powder sugar (one box)
1 stick butter or margarine
3 ounces cream cheese, softened
1/2 teaspoon vanilla
1/4 to 1/2 cup powder baking cocoa

Put all ingredients in Ziploc bag. Squeeze out all the air and start kneading together. It will take about 45 minutes to mix all ingredients thoroughly. You can add peanut butter or substitute mint or other flavorings for the vanilla. This is the basic recipe, so experiment and have fun. Serve by the spoonfuls (can cut the sides of bag after forming a semi-square of fudge and cut into pieces).

The killer part is your hands will get tired if you do this alone. Works best if you have a small group to pass the bag around to so each person can mix the fudge. Very tasty and easy to make.

Elysabeth Eldering, author of the Junior Geography Detective Squad 50-state, mystery trivia series.
http://jgdsseries.blogspot.com
http://junior-geography-detective-squad.weebly.com/

Mean Oatmeal Cookies

Ingredients:

1 cup all-purpose flour
½ tsp baking powder
½ tsp baking soda
¼ tsp salt
1 stick of margarine
½ cup granulated sugar
1/3 cup packed brown sugar
1 egg
2 Tablespoons milk
½ tsp vanilla
2 cups quick-cooking rolled oats (uncooked)

In separate bowl, stir together flour, baking powder, baking soda and salt.

In a mixer bowl, soften and beat margarine for 30 seconds; add sugars and beat until fluffy. Add egg, milk and vanilla; beat well. Add dry ingredients to beaten mixture, beating till well blended. Stir in oats and walnuts.
Chill. Form 1-inch balls and place on ungreased cookie sheet.

If filling is desired, press an indentation in the middle of the cookie and fill the hole halfway with jelly, jam or preserves of choice. Bake at 375° F for 10-12 minutes.

TIP: Cookies are done when they barely begin to turn brown. Anything more than that and they come out too hard. Makes 36 or more.

Mary Deal, author of *River Bones*.
http://www.WriteAnyGenre.com

More Thrilling Than Sex Cake

Ingredients:

1 box yellow cake mix
1 large can pineapple w/juice
1 cup sugar
1 sm pkg instant vanilla pudding, prepared
1 large carton Cool Whip
1 cup of coconut
1 cup of walnuts

Bake cake as directed. While cake is baking simmer pineapple juice and sugar together on stove. When cake is done, poke holes in it and pour mixture over cake. Fold your pudding, Cool Whip, and coconut together and spread over the cake, sprinkle on the nuts and chill. Best if refrigerated overnight.

Anne Patrick, author of the 'Sweet' Edge of Your Seat Romantic Suspense: *Every Skull Tells a Story, Journey to Redemption, Lethal Dreams, Dark Alliance, Ties That Bind, Out of the Darkness, Fire and Ash.*
http://www.suspensebyanne.blogspot.com

Outrageous Hot Chipotle Cake

Ingredients:

10 oz semisweet chocolate, roughly chopped
7 Tbsp unsalted butter, cut into pieces
5 large eggs, room temperature
1 cup sugar
½ tsp chili powder
Dash cayenne pepper
1 tsp cinnamon
Pinch of salt

Preheat the oven to 350° F. Line the bottom of a 9 ½ inch spring-form pan with a circle of parchment paper. Grease the sides and bottom with cooking spray.
Melt the chocolate and butter together over a double boiler or in the microwave, stirring occasionally until smooth.

Whisk together the eggs and the sugar in a large bowl, and then slowly, a bit at a time, whisk in the melted chocolate. Add the salt and spices and taste, adjusting the spices if needed.

Pour into the spring-form pan and bake for 22 to 30 minutes or until a toothpick comes out clean. Let it cool completely on a wire rack. Dust with powdered sugar or serve with whipped cream.

Cindy Sample, author of *The Legacy* and *Dying for a Date*.
www.cindysamplebooks.com

Pistol-Whipped Pecans

Ingredients:

2 cups pecan halves
¾ cup brown sugar
1 egg white (no yolk!)

Whip egg white until frothy. Slowly add light brown sugar. Then mix to coat all pecans. Bake on ungreased cookie sheets 30 minutes at 250° F. The pecans will have a sweet crunchy shell. Yummy!

Susan Whitfield, author of the award-winning Logan Hunter Mystery series: *Genesis Beach, Just North of Luck, Hell Swamp, and Sin Creek.*
www.susanwhitfieldonline.com
www.susanwhitfield.blogspot.com
www.twitter.com/swhitfield

Serial Killer Snicker Doodles

Ingredients:

1 cup softened shortening of your choice (butter, margarine, or Crisco)
1 ½ cups white sugar
2 eggs
2 tsp cream of tartar
1 tsp baking soda
½ tsp salt
1 tsp nutmeg
2 ¾ cups white flour

Cream together the sugar and shortening, then add the eggs and mix well, until somewhat fluffy. Mix the flour, cream of tartar, baking soda, nutmeg, and salt together and then add to the sugar, etc. Roll into walnut sized balls. Roll balls in mixture of ¼ cup cinnamon and ¼ cup sugar. Place unflattened onto ungreased cookie sheet and bake at 350° F 10 to 12 minutes until flat and slightly brown.

This makes many chewy cookies, but the problem comes when you eat them all in serial style, all in one sitting.

Conda V. Douglas, author of *The Dogs of Ubud* in an L&L Dreamspell anthology.
http://condascreativecenter.blogspot.com

Sinful Sweet Potato Pie

Ingredients:

3 lbs sweet potatoes
5 Tbsp melted butter
½ cup + 2 Tbsp brown sugar
½ cup + 1 Tbsp sugar
¼ cup pure maple syrup
2 well beaten eggs
¼ tsp nutmeg
1/8 tsp ground cloves
2/3 tsp cinnamon
1 cup cream or evaporated milk
1 unbaked pie crust

Microwave potatoes whole with skin on, about 16 minutes or until soft.
Scoop out the potatoes into a mixing bowl.
In a mixer, blend potatoes with sugars, eggs, butter, maple syrup, and spices. Blend very well. Add cream and mix until smooth.
Pour mixture into pie crust. Bake for 10 minutes at 400° F. Reduce temperature to 350° F and bake for about 45 minutes until knife comes out clean from center.
Excellent! Freezes well too.

Mark Rosendorf, author of *The Rasner Effect and Without Hesitation: The Rasner Effect II*.
www.markrosendorf.com

Split Banana Cake

Crust ingredients:
1 stick butter
2 cups graham cracker crumbs

Mix and line bottom of large, oblong glass baking dish.
Beat together:
1 box 4X powdered sugar
3 whole eggs
3 sticks margarine
1 tsp vanilla
Smooth mixture over graham cracker base.
Sprinkle 15 oz can crushed pineapple, drained well, over this mixture. Slice 1 or 2 bananas on top of pineapple. Top with whipped topping and sprinkle nuts and cherries on top.

Christy Tillery French, author of *The Bodyguard and The Snitch* and *Chasing Secrets.*
www.christytilleryfrench.com

Suspect Peanut Butter Cookies

Ingredients:

1 cup peanut butter (any brand or style)
1 cup sugar
1 egg

Preheat oven to 350° F. Place all three ingredients in a bowl and stir with a large spoon until well mixed. Scoop out a tablespoon of the dough at a time, roll it into a ball then set on a non-stick cookie sheet. Lightly flour a fork. Use the fork to flatten the cookies in a criss-cross pattern. Place the cookie sheet in the oven and bake until lightly browned. Remove and allow to cool.

If more cookies are desired, double or triple the amount of ingredients listed above.

Janet Durbin, author of *Innocence Taken.*
http://www.janetdurbin.com

Tell-Tale Tortoni

Ingredients:

1/3 cup chopped toasted almonds
3 Tbsp melted butter
1 cup fine vanilla wafer crumbs
1 tsp vanilla
3 pints vanilla ice cream—the square package works best
1 jar (12 oz) apricot preserves

Combine almonds, butter, crumbs, and extract. Mix well. Set aside 1/4 cup crumbs for top. Sprinkle half of remaining crumb mixture over bottom of an 8 inch square pan lined with foil. Spoon half of softened ice cream (if using square package, cut slices of ice cream to fit pan). Drizzle half the preserves and sprinkle with remaining crumb mixture. Repeat. Sprinkle reserved crumb mix over top. Store in freezer until ready to serve. Cut into squares.

Teresa Leigh Judd, author of *Playing House* and *Quick On The Draw*.
www.teresaleighjudd.com

Terrormisu

Ingredients:

1 box chocolate cake mix
2 small boxes chocolate instant pudding
Heath Bars or package of crushed Heath Bar
2 small, 8 oz Cool Whip containers

Bake cake following directions on box. Then make chocolate pudding following the directions on box. Keep pudding at room temperature. Put Heath Bars in zip lock bag and crush with rolling pin, unless using a package of already crushed Heath Bars. Crumble up cake into chunks and set aside. In a large glass trifle serving bowl, layer half of the crumbled cake, half the pudding, 1 Cool Whip container, and half of the Heath bar candy. Repeat layers again. Refrigerate.

Stacy Juba, author of *Twenty-Five Years Ago Today, Sink or Swim, Face-Off* (under Stacy Drumtra).
www.stacyjuba.com

Tipsy Chocolate Truffles

Ingredients:

1 cup dark chocolate candy melts (or use milk chocolate if preferred)
¼ cup whipping cream
2 Tbsp of your favorite wine
1 to 2 cups additional chocolate candy melts for coating

Directions:
Cover a tray with waxed paper.
In a bowl, microwave cream until bubbly and add chocolate candy melts.
Stir until chocolate is melted and well-blended with cream.
Add wine. Stir until well blended.

Refrigerate several hours. Form into ¾ inch balls on paper-lined tray.
Dip in additional melted chocolate coating. Refrigerate.

Makes approximately 24.

Denise Robbins, author of *It Happens In Threes, Killer Bunny Hill,* and *Connect The Dots.*
www.deniserobbins.com

Trifled-With Chocolate

Ingredients:

1 box Devil's Food cake, baked according to the package directions, in two 8 inch round pans
1 - 16 oz container Cool Whip
1 Lg 8 oz Hershey bar with almonds (keep in refrigerator)
1 pkg Brickle bits or 6 Heath candy bars
2 small boxes instant chocolate pudding (prepared)
½ cup coffee or chocolate flavored liqueur

Layer bottom of trifle dish with 1/2 of cake (1 layer broken in pieces). Spoon ¼ cup liqueur on cake. Add ½ of the prepared pudding. Sprinkle ½ package Brickle or Heath bars and ½ Hershey bar broken in pieces over the pudding layer. Spread on a layer of Cool Whip (½ the container). Repeat, ending with Cool Whip layer. Refrigerate until serving.

Cindy Sample, author of *The Legacy* and *Dying for a Date*.
www.cindysamplebooks.com

Unfathomable Flourless Chocolate Cake

Cake ingredients:

12 oz semi-sweet chocolate chips (use ¾ of bag)
2 sticks butter
1 1/3 cups sugar
6 eggs
1 cup unsweetened cocoa powder

Glaze ingredients:

Remaining chocolate chips
3 Tbsp butter
1 Tbsp milk
1 Tbsp corn syrup
½ tsp vanilla

Preheat oven to 375° F.

Spray 9 inch round pan with nonstick spray. Line with circle of waxed paper. Spray paper. Add ¾ bag of chips to medium saucepan. Add 2 sticks of butter. Melt over low heat, stirring often until completely blended. Remove from heat and pour into a large bowl. Add sugar and mix well. Add one egg at a time, whisking into the mixture before adding another. Sift cocoa powder into the bowl. Stir until blended. Pour batter into baking pan. Bake for 30-35 minutes or until a thin crust forms and cake has risen. The cake will be firm in the center. Cool cake.

For glaze, pour remaining chocolate chips into a saucepan. Melt with butter over low heat. Stir until blended. Remove from heat. Add milk, syrup, and vanilla. Set aside.

Pour glaze over cooled cake and spread evenly. Chill for one hour before serving.

Michelle Hollstein-Matkins, author of The Aggie Underhill Mysteries.
www.MichelleAnnHollstein.com

Walloped Black Jack Pie

Ingredients:

2 cups cold milk
2 Tbsp Jack Daniel's (Black Label) Tennessee Sour Mash Whiskey
1 - 6 oz serving of vanilla instant pudding
2 tsp instant coffee (press granules between waxed paper to pulverize)
1 baked pastry or graham cracker pie crust or a dozen baked pastry tart shells

Pour milk and whiskey into deep narrow-bottom bowl. Add pudding mix and instant coffee.

Beat slowly with rotary beater or one minute on low with mixer. Pour into pie crust.

Chill at least 3 hours; top with whipped cream and sprinkle with cinnamon or freshly grated nutmeg if desired.

Keith Donnelly, author of the Donald Youngblood Mystery series: *Three Deuces Down* and *Three Days Dead*.
www.donaldyoungbloodmysteries.com

Warped Whoopee Pies

Ingredients:

½ cup solid vegetable shortening
1 cup firmly packed brown sugar
1 egg
¼ cup cocoa
2 cups all-purpose flour
1 tsp baking powder
1 tsp baking soda
1 tsp salt
1 tsp vanilla extract
1 cup milk

Preheat oven to 350° F. Lightly grease baking sheets.
In a large bowl, cream together shortening, sugar, and egg. In another bowl, combine cocoa, flour, baking powder, baking soda, and salt. In a small bowl, stir the vanilla extract into the milk. Add the dry ingredients to the shortening mixture, alternating with the milk mixture, beating until smooth. Drop batter by the ¼ cup (to make 18 cakes) onto prepared baking sheets. With the back of a spoon spread batter into 4-inch circles, leaving approximately 2 inches between each cake. Bake 15 minutes or until they are firm to the touch. Remove from oven and let cool completely on a wire rack.

Filling:

1 cup solid vegetable shortening
1 ½ cups powdered sugar
2 cups Marshmallow Fluff
1 ½ teaspoons vanilla extract

In a medium bowl, beat together shortening, sugar, and Marshmallow fluff; stir in vanilla extract until well blended. When the cakes are completely cool, spread the flat side (bottom) of one chocolate cake with a generous amount of filling. Top with another cake, pressing down gently to distribute the filling evenly. Repeat with all cookies to make 9 pies. Wrap whoopee pies individually in plastic wrap, or place them in a single layer on a platter (do not stack them, as they tend to stick). You can freeze them the same way, by wrapping each pie in plastic wrap and putting them in a freezer proof container. Thaw them again in the fridge.

Bente Gallagher (Jennie Bentley), author of *Fatal Fixer-Upper, Spackled and Spooked,* and *Plaster and Poison.* www.jenniebentley.com

Wicked Strawberry Pie

Ingredients:

4 oz cream cheese (softened)
1 Tbsp milk
1 Tbsp lemon juice
4 tsp sugar or 2 packets artificial sweetener
1 12 oz container Cool Whip
1 quart fresh strawberries
2 small pkg instant vanilla pudding
2 cups milk
2 graham cracker crusts

Beat cream cheese with 1 Tbsp milk until creamy. Add sugar or artificial sweetener and mix well then add lemon juice. Fold in 2/3 of the Cool Whip and spread into the pie crusts. Slice half of the strawberries on top. Set aside. Mix 2 cups milk with the vanilla pudding mix. Fold in the rest of the Cool Whip and pour on top of the pies. Refrigerate overnight or for at least 4 hours. Garnish with fresh strawberries.

Caitlyn Hunter, author of *The Secret Life of Alice Smitty* in an L&L Dreamspell anthology.
http://caitlynhunter.com

Insane Soups, Salads, and Sauces

BLACK EYED
SALAD

Assassin's Apple Cabbage Soup

Ingredients:

1 Tbsp olive oil
1 onion
3 carrots
3 cups vegetable stock
1 cup water
2 cups apple cider
¼ cup brown sugar
3 cinnamon sticks
3 apples (any variety)
½ tsp ground nutmeg
½ head cabbage (large) or 1 medium cabbage
½ tsp pepper

Place stockpot on stove over medium heat. Add oil. Chop onion into small pieces. Add to oil and cook for about five minutes, stirring frequently. Cut carrots into small pieces, also add to oil, and cook an additional five minutes.

Add vegetable stock, apple cider, water, brown sugar, and cinnamon sticks and turn heat up to medium high. Meanwhile peel and chop apples into pieces small enough to fit on a spoon.

Once liquid comes to boil, add apples. Sprinkle liquid with nutmeg and pepper and stir. Chop cabbage into small pieces, and add that to liquid. Bring liquid back to boil once again.

Once liquid boils, lower to a simmer. Simmer for 15 to 20 minutes, or until apples are tender. Spoon out into bowls and serve.

James Mascia, author of *High School Heroes*.
www.islandofdren.com

Black-Eyed Salad

Ingredients:

2 - 15 ½ oz cans black eye peas, drained and rinsed
1 small bell pepper, finely chopped
1 small onion, finely chopped

Toss all ingredients with ½ cup fat free Italian dressing. Allow to set overnight if possible. Serve.

Susan Whitfield, author of the award-winning Logan Hunter Mystery series: *Genesis Beach, Just North of Luck, Hell Swamp, and Sin Creek.*
www.susanwhitfieldonline.com
www.susanwhitfield.blogspot.com
www.twitter.com/swhitfield

Bueno New Mexican Posole

Ingredients:

1 lb frozen posole (uncooked hominy)
1 envelope dry onion soup
1 can chicken broth
2 Tbsp medium green or red chilies, chopped
¼ tsp crushed red chile pepper
½ tsp chopped garlic
3 cups water
3 to 5 tsp chicken bouillon or 3 to 5 bouillon cubes
½ onion, diced
½ lb pork cut into ½ inch cubes
1 tsp olive oil

Heat olive oil in 2 or 3 quart sauce pan over med heat, add onion and garlic and simmer for 3 to 4 minutes. Add pork and brown well. Add chicken broth, onion soup, chile peppers, crushed chile, water, and bouillon. Bring to simmer. Add posole, bring to a boil and reduce heat to simmer for about 1 hour or until the posole has softened. Adjust bouillon or add salt and pepper to taste. Note: the longer you cook any chile, the hotter it becomes. If the soup becomes too spicy, add more broth.

Penny Rudolph, author of *The Eye of the Mountain God, Thicker Than Blood, Lifeblood, and Listen to the Mockingbird.*
www.pennyrudolph.com

Chilling Corn Salad

Ingredients:

2 - 16 oz cans white shoe peg corn, drained
1 - 2 oz jar pimentos, drained
½ cup green peppers, chopped
½ cup onion, chopped
2 stalks celery, chopped
½ cup vegetable oil
½ cup white vinegar
1 tsp salt
½ tsp pepper
½ cup sugar

Combine vegetables, tossing lightly. Combine remaining ingredients. Mix well. Pour over vegetables and toss. Cover and chill overnight.
Drain before serving.
Serves 6.

Lynette Hall Hampton, author of *Stetson Mold* and the Reverend Willa Hinshaw series.
www.lynettehallhampton.com

Don's Caesar Salad

Featured in *Three Deuces Down*

Ingredients:

Hearts of Romaine lettuce, washed, dried, and broken into small bite-size pieces
Cardini's bottled dressing—the original Caesar dressing (or your own favorite)
Aged Italian Parmigiano Reggiano cheese block
Homemade croutons (see below)
Freshly ground black pepper
One anchovy

Grind anchovy around the bottom and sides of a jumbo salad bowl deep enough for tossing lettuce. Remove any anchovy pieces. Put lettuce pieces in the bowl; add just enough dressing to lightly coat the leaves, toss gently. Grate or slice fresh cheese in large slivers into bowl along with croutons, being sure to crush a few croutons into crumbs to spread through the salad to enhance flavor. Gently toss; add black pepper before serving. Adding tiny bits of anchovy is also an option.

Homemade Croutons:
Preheat oven to 350° F. Any bread that is not extremely fresh will do; in fact a variety of bread makes better tasting croutons! Cut into desired size cubes to make about 4 cups. Melt ½ stick of butter and mix with 1 Tbsp of Lawry's Pinch of Herbs Classic Herb Blend. In large bowl, toss cubes and butter mixture until coated. Spread bread cubes on cookie sheet and bake for 10 to 15 minutes, until browned and crusty. Spread on absorbent paper to cool.

Keith Donnelly, author of the Donald Youngblood Mystery series: *Three Deuces Down* and *Three Days Dead*.
www.donaldyoungbloodmysteries.com

Drowned Fish Chowder

Ingredients:

2 lb firm white fish, cut in bite-sized chunks (I generally use frozen cod)
4 potatoes, diced
½ cup celery leaves
1 bay leaf
2 ½ tsp salt
½ tsp cayenne (or more)
1 tsp chili powder
2 to 4 garlic cloves, minced
4 large onions, diced
½ cup butter (leave out if using Half and Half)
¼ tsp dill seed
¼ tsp pepper
2 cups Half and Half (or milk)
Chopped parsley for garnish
½ cup white wine or Rose'
2 cups boiling water

Preheat oven to 375° F. Put all the ingredients except the cream and the parsley into a 3 quart Dutch oven or casserole. Cover tightly. Bake one hour or until potatoes are soft. Heat cream (milk, half and half, whatever) and add. Garnish with parsley.

If you want to get fancy, add shrimp and/or scallops at the last minute, being careful not to overcook them. Sautéed mushrooms, a little green pepper, frozen corn all work if you want to stretch the soup a little. Makes 2 ½ quarts.

Vicki Lane, author of the Elizabeth Goodweather series: *Old Wounds, Signs in the Blood, Art's Blood,* and *In A Dark Season.*
www.vickilane.com

Feisty Mandarin Chicken Salad

Ingredients:

1 cup chicken, cubed and cooked
4 cups lettuce/salad greens
1 - 11 oz can mandarin oranges, drained
¼ cup vegetable oil
2 Tbsp sugar
¼ tsp pepper
¼ cup red onion, sliced
¼ cup almonds, slivered and browned in butter
2 Tbsp wine vinegar
½ tsp salt

Dressing: combine oil, vinegar, sugar, salt, and pepper. Set aside in refrigerator. Mix together chicken, lettuce, onions, mandarin oranges, and almonds. When ready to serve, toss salad with dressing.

Susanne Marie Knight, author of *Competitors*.
www.susanneknight.com

Feuding New Mexico Black Bean Soup

Ingredients:

1 Tbsp olive oil
½ cup chopped onions
¼ cup sliced celery
1½ tsp ground cumin
¾ tsp ground cilantro
¼ tsp coriander
¼ tsp crushed chile
2 – 14 oz cans black beans, drained and rinsed
1 – 14 oz can diced tomatoes
1½ cups water
1 envelope dry onion soup
1 tsp salsa
¼ cup light sour cream
¼ cup finely chopped green onions

Heat oil in saucepan over medium high heat. Sauté the ½ cup onions 4 to 5 minutes or until onion turns golden. Stir in celery, cumin, cilantro, coriander, crushed chile. Add black beans, tomatoes, water, onion soup, and salsa. Bring to boil, reduce heat to simmer 20 minutes, stirring frequently. Serve soup with a dollop of sour cream and sprinkled with the finely chopped onions.

Penny Rudolph, author of *Thicker Than Blood, Lifeblood, Eye of the Mountain God* and *Listen to the Mockingbird.*
www.pennyrundolph.com

Illegally Easy Salad

This is more or less one where you grab enough handfuls of stuff to feed the number of people who are dining, so it's more an ingredients list than something carefully measured.

Spring Mix prepackaged salad mix
A handful or more of trail mix that includes dried fruits
¼ cup orange flavored dried cranberries
¼ cup walnuts or almonds (optional)

Mix with enough Asian Sesame dressing to dampen the greens—don't drown them.

Morgan St. James, author *A Corpse in the Soup, Seven Deadly Samovars, The World Outside The Window,* and *Saying Goodbye To Miss Molly.*
www.morganstjames-author.com
www.silversistersmysteries.com

Lawless Lexie's Taco Salad

Ingredients:

1 head of lettuce, torn into bite size pieces
1 pound of ground beef, browned and drained
1 bag of Fritos
1 bottle of Russian dressing
1 - 8 oz bag of shredded sharp cheddar cheese
3 chopped tomatoes
1 chopped onion
1 - 8 oz container of sour cream
1 package of taco seasoning

Brown ground beef, drain, and mix with taco seasoning according to the packet's instructions. Toss lettuce with Fritos, shredded cheese, tomatoes, and onion. Drizzle dressing as desired and top with a dollop of sour cream. Serves 4.

Cindy Keen Reynders, author of The Saucy Lucy Mysteries, and *Paws-itively Guilty.*
www.cindykeenreynders.com

Malevolent Buffalo Chicken Soup

Ingredients:

1 Tbsp vegetable oil
1 medium/large onion
3 boneless skinless chicken breasts
2 ½ cups chicken stock
1 tsp powdered garlic
1 tsp pepper
1 - 15 oz can condensed cheddar cheese soup
¼ cup buffalo wing sauce
Crumbled blue cheese

Put stockpot on stove over medium heat. Add oil and let warm. Meanwhile, chop onion into ½ inch pieces. Add chopped onion to oil. Cook for 5 minutes, constantly stirring until onions appear translucent.

Cut chicken breasts into 1 inch cubes. Add to stockpot and stir in with onions.

Let chicken cook for about 1 minute, and then add chicken stock. Raise to medium/high heat and let stock come to a boil.

Turn heat to low. Add cheddar cheese soup and stir until well mixed.

Stir in garlic and pepper. Then stir in buffalo wing sauce. Let simmer for 5 minutes.

Spoon into bowls, garnish with blue cheese and serve hot.

James Mascia, author of *High School Heroes.*
www.islandofdren.com

Paws-itively Guilty Goulash

Ingredients:

3 cups macaroni
2 teaspoons minced garlic
½ cup minced onion
2 sprigs parsley (optional)
½ cup mushrooms
1 pound ground beef
2 - 14 ½ oz cans of whole tomatoes, undrained
1 - 6 oz can tomato paste

Boil macaroni in salted water, drain, and set aside. Brown hamburger in skillet, drain, and add garlic, onion, parsley, mushrooms, tomatoes and tomato paste. Cook 40 minutes and pour over macaroni. Serves 4.

Cindy Keen Reynders, author of The Saucy Lucy Mysteries and *Paws-itively Guilty.*
www.cindykeenreynders.com

Potent Vegetarian Taco Soup

Ingredients:

1 large can crushed tomatoes
1 onion
1 can refried beans
1 packet or 3 Tbsp taco seasoning
¼ cup fresh salsa
1 can vegetable stock
1 cup water
1 Tbsp garlic powder
1 Tbsp black pepper
2 cups cheddar cheese
Sour cream
Crushed tortilla chips
2 Tbsp olive oil

Put stockpot on stove over medium heat. Pour oil into pot. Chop onions into small pieces (about the same size as the chunks in whatever salsa you're using) and cook for 6 to 8 minutes, stirring frequently.

Once onions have cooked, add can of crushed tomatoes, vegetable stock and water. Stir. Add taco seasoning, garlic, pepper, and salsa. Raise heat to high and bring soup to a boil, stirring frequently. Once soup boils, lower heat again to medium and add refried beans. Stir until bean mixture dissolves.

Simmer soup for 15 minutes. Turn heat off. Take 1 ½ cups of cheddar cheese and stir into soup. Spoon soup into bowls. Dab some sour cream in the center of soup and top with a sprinkle of cheddar cheese and crushed tortilla chips.

James Mascia, author of *High School Heroes*.
www.islandofdren.com

Pretzeled Salad

Ingredients:

1 stick margarine
¼ cup sugar
1 ½ cups crushed pretzels
1 large package strawberry Jell-O (sugar-free)
2 cups boiling water
2 - 10 oz packages frozen strawberries
8 oz cream cheese
8 oz Cool Whip
1 cup sugar

Mix margarine, ¼ cup sugar, and crushed pretzels. Press in 13" x 9" pan. Bake at 350° F for 5 minutes, let cool. Mix together cream cheese, Cool Whip, and 1 cup sugar. Spread on cooled crust. Dissolve strawberry Jell-O in 2 cups boiling water. Stir in frozen strawberries. Pour over cream cheese layer. Chill overnight.

Christy Tillery French, author of *The Bodyguard and the Snitch, The Bodyguard and the Rock Star, The Bodyguard and the Show Dog, The Bodyguard, and Chasing Horses*.
http://christytilleryfrench.com
http://damesofdialogue.wordpress.com

Sherbet Smoothie Salad

Dissolve: 2 pks orange Jell-O in 1 cup hot water

Add: 1 pint orange sherbet & stir until dissolved. Then add 1 15 ½ oz can crushed pineapple with juice and 1 small can mandarin oranges. Mix well and let set until firm.

Topping: 2 beaten eggs, 1 cup pineapple juice or orange juice, and 2 Tbsp flour.

Mix together and cook on medium heat until thick. Cool.

Fold in 1 small container of Cool Whip. Let set until firm. This is rather elegant and nice to take to Pitch In Dinners.

Marilyn Gardiner, author of the Winsom series: *Dancing Ladies, Window On Windemere, Banjo Eyes,* and *Mistletoe and Holly.* http://marilyn-gardiner.com

Snake Dance Marinade

Ingredients:

2 - 8 oz steaks
¼ cup Balsamic vinegar
¼ cup Italian dressing
Fresh ground black pepper
1 tsp sea salt or Kosher salt
1 tsp crushed fresh garlic
1 tsp red pepper flakes

Add ¼ cup Balsamic vinegar to large bowl with tight lid. Add ¼ cup Italian dressing. Sprinkle and or fresh grind black pepper to taste. Add one teaspoon of sea salt or Kosher salt. I like both, so if you add both, half a teaspoon each. Add crushed fresh garlic and red pepper flakes. Stir. Place steak and/or steaks into the marinade. Cover 2 to 4 hours. Start grill. Place marinated meat on the grill. Grill to your liking.

Angelica Hart and Zi, author of *Killer Dolls, Snake Dance,* and *Chasing Gravitas.*
www.angelicahartandzi.com

Tainted Taco Soup

Cook time: 8 hours in slow cooker

Ingredients:

1 pound ground beef (browned)
1 onion, chopped
1 - 16 oz can chili beans, with liquid (mild)
1 - 15 oz can kidney beans, drained
1 - 15 oz can whole kernel corn, with liquid
1 - 8 oz can tomato sauce
2 - 14.5 oz cans diced tomatoes with green chili peppers (mild)
1 package taco seasoning
1 package ranch seasoning mix

Put all ingredients in slower cooker and mix well. Cook on low for 8 hours. Serve topped with shredded cheese, sour cream, and tortilla chips. (Recipe used with Tracy Scott's permission.)

J.J. Keller, author of *Trade Agreement.*
www.jj-keller.com
http://www.lyricalpress.com/jj_keller

Tetchy Garlic Tomato Sauce

Ingredients:

1 Tbsp garlic powder
6 cloves garlic
2 cans crushed tomatoes
2 onions
1 Tbsp dried basil
1 Tbsp dried oregano
1 Tbsp garlic powder
1 can tomato paste
1 Tbsp olive oil
1 Tbsp pepper
Pasta (any variety)

Place stockpot on stove over medium heat. Add oil. Chop onion into small pieces and add to pan. Cook at least 7 minutes, stirring frequently. Meanwhile, peel and slice three of the cloves of garlic into large slivers. Add those to the pan and cook 2 more minutes, stirring frequently. Take the remaining garlic cloves, and press out into pan. Cook 1 more minute. Add two cans of crushed tomatoes and can of tomato paste and stir. Add garlic powder, pepper, basil, and oregano and continue to stir. Raise heat to medium high and bring sauce to a boil, stirring frequently.

Once sauce boils, lower to a simmer and cook for at least 40 minutes, stirring frequently.
Pour over any pasta you wish, toss, and serve.

James Mascia, author of *High School Heroes*.
www.islandofdren.com

Torn Spinach and Berry Salad

Ingredients:

8 cups fresh spinach, washed well and torn into bite-size pieces
2 cups fresh strawberries, washed and sliced
1 cup fresh blueberries, washed
½ cup spiced pecans
Shredded coconut for garnish

Dressing:
½ cup sour cream
¼ cup honey
2 tsp lime juice
1/8 tsp nutmeg

Gently toss spinach and berries in salad bowl; refrigerate.
Chop spiced pecans and set aside. In small bowl, combine all
dressing ingredients; blend well. Cover and refrigerate to blend
flavors. Serve with dressing, tossing if desired. Garnish with
coconut and spiced pecan bits (below). Makes 8 servings.

Spiced Pecans:
½ tsp ground cumin
½ tsp Cayenne powder
½ tsp ground cinnamon
¼ tsp ground nutmeg
½ cup butter
¼ cup brown sugar
2 Tbsp vinegar
2 cups shelled pecan halves

Preheat oven to 300° F.

Mix spices in a small bowl. Melt butter in a saucepan and add brown sugar. Stir until sugar melts. Add vinegar. Stir until all dry ingredients are dissolved. Toss nuts into the saucepan and coat with spice mixture. Line a cookie sheet with aluminum foil. Place the pecan halves on the sheet in one layer. Bake 15 minutes, removing every 5 minutes to flip pecans over with a spatula. Don't let them burn! Remove from oven and let cool for 2 hours without covering, so that the nuts will become crisp when they cool. Store in airtight jars or tins.

Cash Anthony, author of *Yes, She Bites, A Bona Fide Quirk in the Law, The Best Man,* and *The Stand-In* in L&L Dreamspell's anthologies, also short films and screenplays.
www.lldreamspell.com

Wicked Tomato Basil Soup

Ingredients:

1 chopped onion
1 large can drained diced tomatoes
½ can tomato paste
½ cup fine sugar
1 Tbsp chopped thyme
1 Tbsp chopped basil
2 cups chicken stock (use the boxed variety)

Sauté onions in margarine or butter until soft but not brown.
Add drained tomatoes to onions and sauté well.
Add tomato paste and mix well.
Add sugar and spices.
Add chicken broth.
Cook on medium/low for 20 minutes.
Let cool.
Pour mixture into blender and puree all ingredients together.
Pour into saucepan. Add ½ cup cream.

You may add cooked Orzo to the pureed soup. Serve with a basil leaf in the middle of the bowl. Can also be served with a dollop of sour cream.
Delicious! Freezes well.

Mark Rosendorf, author of *The Rasner Effect* and *Without Hesitation: The Rasner Effect II.*
www.markrosendorf.com

Shameless Sides

MEAN McLEAN'S FAMOUS MAC 'N CHEESE

Battered Vegetable Pancakes

Ingredients:

1 batch of pancake batter (I use Bisquick, starting with 2 cups of dry mix)
1 cup shredded carrots
1 cup shredded zucchini
Applesauce
Shredded cheddar cheese

Divide pancake batter into two bowls. Add shredded carrots to one bowl and shredded zucchini to another and mix each bowl well. Cook pancakes and serve with applesauce and cheese on top.

Beth Groundwater, author of *A Real Basket Case* (Best First Novel Agatha Award nominee), and *To Hell In A Handbasket*.
http://bethgroundwater.com

Bleeding Hawaiian Breadfruit

Ingredients:

1 large Hawaiian breadfruit
Hawaiian salt (red or white) to taste
2 bay leaves
Fresh garlic or garlic powder, to taste
2 small red Hawaiian chili peppers (optional)

Pick breadfruit by its color: Good ones are hard and yellowish, with brown spots. If soft, they are too ripe. After picking, put on the ground for a few minutes to let it bleed. Don't get the fluid on you. It's sticky. Cut off both ends, stand upright.

Cut the skin off. Quarter it and remove the core. Boil in large pot for 45 minutes to 1 hour or till tender. It will float. Into the water, add Hawaiian salt, bay leaves, fresh garlic or garlic powder, and small red Hawaiian chili peppers. When done, remove from water (discard water), slice, and serve with butter. It's good, too, with salt and pepper.

Save leftovers in a plastic bag in the refrigerator. Can be reheated and served with butter.
Many Hawaiians slice the cooked fruit and eat with butter and syrup, like pancakes.
One large breadfruit easily serves four or more.

Alternate Recipe:

Mash one quarter cooked breadfruit, and then mix with corned beef and onion, salt and pepper. Fry until meat is done. Serves 1-2.

Mary Deal, author of *River Bones*.
www.WriteAnyGenre.com

Cantankerous Corn Pudding

Ingredients:

1 can creamed corn
1 can regular corn
½ stick margarine
¼ cup sugar
3 eggs
½ cup flour
1 tsp baking powder
3/4 cup cream
1 tsp vanilla

Mix all ingredients together with creamed corn. Add regular corn. Bake at 350° F for 1 hour.

Mark Rosendorf, author of *The Rasner Effect* and *Without Hesitation: The Rasner Effect II.*
www.markrosendorf.com

Deadline Pintos & Corn Bread

Ingredients:

1 med onion, chopped
1 med green bell pepper, chopped
3 cloves garlic, minced (or ¼ tsp garlic powder)

Sauté the above ingredients in 1 Tbsp oil until onions and garlic are tender. Then place into a crock-pot and add:
2 cans pinto beans, drained
16 oz can diced tomatoes, with juice
8 oz can tomato sauce
½ tsp chili powder
½ tsp black pepper
½ tsp prepared mustard
½ tsp red pepper flakes

Stir and let cook for 1½ hours on high. Then in a bowl combine:
1 cup yellow cornmeal
1 cup all-purpose flour
2 ½ tsp baking powder
½ tsp salt
1 ½ Tbsp sugar

After the dry ingredients are combined, add to bowl:
3/4 cup soy milk
2 eggs
2 Tbsp vegetable oil
1 can cream corn

Mix well, and then spoon over the bean mix in the crock-pot. Cover and cook on high for an additional 2 hours. Serves 6.

Raven Bower, author of *Apparitions*.
www.ravenbower.com

Deviled Eggs

Ingredients:

12 eggs
3 Tbsp Hellmanns's Real Mayonnaise
2 Tbsp French's Mustard
1 cup Vlasic sweet gherkin pickles
¼ cup pickle juice
½ tsp salt
½ tsp pepper

Boil eggs for 10 minutes. Remove from heat and place in cold water. Cool them thoroughly. While eggs are cooling, chop finely 1 cup of sweet pickles. Then cut eggs into halves, removing the yellow yolk. Set halves aside for now. Take yellow yolks, mayonnaise, mustard, finely chopped sweet pickles, ½ tsp salt, ½ tsp of pepper, and pour ¼ cup of pickle juice into mix, stir until all ingredients are mixed well. Then take mix and heap into the egg halves. Chill 2 hours.

Melinda Elmore, author of *Ghosts of Sand Creek*.
www.melindaelmore.webs.com

Freaky Fried Apples

Ingredients:

4 to 6 tart apples, cut into wedges
2 cups sugar
1 Tbsp oil
1 ½ cups water

Use heavy skillet. Combine water, oil, sugar, and bring to boil. Add apples. Cook on fairly high heat without a lid until apples are clear, about 15 minutes. Add small amount of water if needed to keep syrupy.

Susan Whitfield, author of the award-winning Logan Hunter Mystery series: *Genesis Beach, Just North of Luck, Hell Swamp, and Sin Creek.*
www.susanwhitfieldonline.com
www.susanwhitfield.blogspot.com
www.twitter.com/swhitfield

Garroted Garlic-Zucchini-Potato Pancakes

Ingredients:

6 cloves of garlic—or more
1 zucchini
2 potatoes
Packaged pancake mix (or multi-purpose pancake/biscuit mix)
1 cup milk
2 eggs
Oil

Wash the potatoes, remove any bad spots, then microwave until they're baked, remove "meat" from the skin, place in a bowl and mash with a fork.

Peel and press the garlic.Wash and grate zucchini. Place in a pan with 2 Tbsp olive oil and sauté until tender.

Stir into potato mixture, and then follow directions for a batch of pancakes (2 cups of dry mix, two eggs and about 1 cup of milk), adjusting liquid to the batter consistency you want.

Cook on a griddle as you would regular pancakes.

Serve for brunch, lunch, or dinner with butter, sour cream, and salsa.

Carolyn Rose, author of *Hemlock Lake* and co-author of *The Big Grabowski.*
www.krillbooks.com

Horsing-Around Slaw

For those who don't like slaw.

Ingredients:

2 radishes, sliced
¼ onion, sliced
Red cabbage, a couple thin slices, chopped
½ apple, sliced
¼ orange, peeled and sections cut in slices
½ banana, sliced
1 tsp lemon juice
1 tsp honey
1 to 1 ½ tsp horseradish sauce
¼ cup light mayonnaise

Mix and serve.

Penny Rudolph, award-winning author of *Thicker Than Blood,
Lifeblood, Listen to the Mockingbird, and Eye of the Mountain God.*
www.PennyRudolph.com

Insomniac's Overnight Coleslaw

Ingredients:

12 cups shredded cabbage (1 medium head)
1 green pepper, chopped
1 medium red onion, chopped
2 carrots, shredded
1 cup sugar

Dressing:
2 tsp sugar
1 tsp dry mustard
1 tsp celery seed
1 tsp salt
1 cup vinegar
¾ cup vegetable oil

In a large bowl, combine first four ingredients. Sprinkle with sugar; set aside.
In a saucepan, combine dressing ingredients; bring to a boil. Remove from the heat and pour over vegetables, stirring to cover evenly. Cover and refrigerate overnight. Stir well before serving. Yield: 12 to 16 servings.

H. L. Chandler, author of *The Keepers*.
http://www.hlchandler.bravehost.com

Mean McLean's Famous Mac 'N Cheese

Ingredients:

1 - 7 oz package Creamettes
½ cup butter or margarine
1 ½ cups sharp cheddar cheese
1 ½ cups evaporated milk
2 Tbsp flour
1 tsp salt
¼ tsp pepper

Cook Creamettes as directed on package. Melt butter over low heat and stir into flour to form a smooth paste. Add milk, stirring constantly. Add salt and pepper and cook until thickened. Remove from heat. Place drained Creamettes in greased bake dish and mix in ½ the cheese. Reheat sauce and mix with macaroni and cheese. Sprinkle heavily with rest of cheese and dot with 2 Tbsp of butter. Bake 20 to 25 minutes in 300° F oven. If crust is desired (and it would be a shame not to have it) place in broiler for a few minutes or until brown.

Slather on plate and do not be shy about asking for seconds. Next day leftovers are great in the microwave. Fill paper plate with Mac 'n cheese, cover with second paper plate, and zap for 1½ to 2 minutes. (Recipe used with Rosie McLean's permission.)

J D Webb, award-winning author *of Shepherd's Pie, Moon Over Chicago, Her Name Is Mommy,* and *Smudge.*
www.jdwebb.com

Naughty Noodle Pudding

Ingredients:

1 package wide noodles
1 tsp vanilla
Craisins
Corn flakes
Cinnamon
½ cup sugar
¾ cup milk
4 eggs
8 oz sour cream
8 oz cottage cheese
½ stick butter
Small can crushed pineapple

Blend together cheese, sour cream, sugar, eggs, vanilla, milk, and butter. Mix with cooked noodles and add pineapple and craisins. Put mixture in baking casserole dish. Sprinkle cinnamon on top. Sprinkle crushed corn flakes on top.
Bake at 375° F for 45 minutes.

Mark Rosendorf, author of *The Rasner Effect* and *Without Hesitation: The Rasner Effect II*.
www.markrosendorf.com

Peppered Relish

Ingredients:

12 green bell peppers
12 red bell peppers
12 Vidalia onions
1 box brown sugar
3 Tbsp salt
1 pint white vinegar

Prepare canning jars: wash jars thoroughly and turn down on roasting pan with 1 inch of water. Stick into 400° F oven and sterilize. Have lids boiling in pan on stove. Have rings nearby.

Grind peppers in food processor or "Handy Chop" and add salt. Boil 5 minutes. Simmer 10 minutes. Drain. Add sugar and vinegar. Boil 5 more minutes. Ladle into hot jars. (Note: I have also mixed in orange and yellow peppers and it's beautiful. Easy recipe once peppers are ground.) Serve on field peas or collard greens.

Susan Whitfield, author of the award-winning Logan Hunter Mystery series: *Genesis Beach, Just North of Luck, Hell Swamp, and Sin Creek.*
www.susanwhitfieldonline.com
www.susanwhitfield.blogspot.com
www.twitter.com/swhitfield

Plunger Mayonnaise

My mother and grandmother and my mother-in-law too all had special mayonnaise makers—tall glass cylinders with the recipe embossed on them and with metal plungers. These recipes called for egg yolks only. This recipe is a slight adaptation, suited to a blender.

2 eggs
A pinch or more of cayenne pepper (to taste)
1 tsp prepared mustard (my folks used yellow; I use Dijon)
Juice of one fresh lemon (about 4 Tbsp)
1 tsp salt
1 tsp sugar
2 cups canola oil

Put all ingredients, except for 1 ¾ cup oil, into blender. Blend 5 seconds on low. Keep blender running and add remaining oil in a slow thin stream. Stop blender and stir mayo with rubber spatula, scraping the sides well. Blend again until good consistency.

Vicki Lane, author of the Elizabeth Goodweather Mystery series: *Old Wounds, Signs in the Blood, Art's Blood,* and *In A Dark Season.* www.vickilane.com

Slippery Elbows

Ingredients:

2 cups dry elbow macaroni
½ stick butter or margarine
Celery to taste
Salt to taste
Black pepper to taste, if desired

Cook elbows until done, drain. While hot, melt in the butter or margarine right in the pot. Stir for a good slippery mix. Season to taste.

Mary Deal, author of *River Bones*.
www.WriteAnyGenre.com

Vampire-free Pasta

For garlic lovers

Ingredients:

1 lb package angel hair pasta, cooked
1 bulb garlic, finely chopped
1 onion, finely chopped
½ cup grated Parmesan cheese
¼ cup olive oil
¼ tsp crushed hot pepper
1 tsp dried parsley
Salt and pepper to taste

Sauté the onions and garlic in the olive oil until translucent. When you can stake the garlic with a fork, remove pan from heat and dump into your hot pasta. Mix well. Add salt, parsley, pepper, and crushed pepper. Then sprinkle in the Parmesan cheese a bit at a time.

Serves 6.

Raven Bower, author of *Apparitions*.
www.ravenbower.com

Whipped Spezerillo

Ingredients:

1 lb smallest pasta with a hole in it, cooked
1 - 20 oz can pineapple bits
1 - 20 oz can pineapple, crushed
2 - 11 oz cans mandarin oranges

Drain all fruit into a measuring cup to get 1 ¾ cup juice then pour into a pan and add:
2 cups sugar
¾ cup flour
3 eggs
¼ tsp salt

Stir constantly and bring to boil until thick and pudding-like. Then cool.

Once pasta and pudding have cooled, mix together along with drained fruit. Then add:
1 - 10 oz pkg. mini marshmallows (I don't use the entire bag)
1 - 9 oz container Cool Whip

Mix all ingredients in large bowl and refrigerate overnight.

Denise Robbins, author of *It Happens In Threes, Killer Bunny Hill, and Connect The Dots.*
www.deniserobboins.com

CLANDESTINE CHEESE PUFFS

Slayer Casseroles

CRIMINAL CHICKEN CHILE CASSEROLE

Corn Pone Pie

1 lb ground beef, browned
1/3 cup chopped onions
1 Tbsp olive oil
1 cup whole kernel corn
1 ½ cans (14.2 oz size can) chopped tomatoes
2 tsp chili powder (or less)
½ teaspoon salt
1 tsp Worcestershire Sauce
1 can kidney beans, drained
1 package Jiffy Cornbread Mix

Brown hamburger and onions in oil. Add seasonings and tomatoes. Cover and simmer for a few minutes. Add beans and pour into greased 8" x 8" inch casserole. Top with 1 package Jiffy cornbread mix, made as directed on box. (Spread with a wet knife.) Bake at 425° F for 20-25 minutes.

Marilyn Gardiner, author of the Winsom series: *Dancing Ladies, Window On Windemere, Banjo Eyes,* and *Mistletoe & Holly.*
http://marilyn-gardiner.com

Criminal Chicken-Chile Casserole

Ingredients:

3 or 4 chicken breasts, cooked and shredded
1 medium onion
1 zucchini
2 carrots
1 can cream of mushroom soup
1 cup sour cream
1 to 2 cups shredded sharp cheddar cheese or a mixture of cheddar and jack cheese
1 cup chopped green chilies (canned, fresh, or frozen)
Corn tortillas
Crushed corn chips

Chop and sauté onion, carrot, and zucchini in a little oil until tender. (You can add mushrooms, too, or substitute other veggies.) Place in a large bowl with shredded chicken, soup (undiluted), sour cream, cheese, and green chilies (or sauté jalapeno peppers or other hot peppers of your choice and in the amount you can tolerate). Add enough water to make the mixture spreadable, but not soupy.

Oil a 9" x 13" baking pan and spread corn tortillas on the bottom. Spread on about 1/3 of chicken/chile mixture and layer on more tortillas. Repeat, and then cover the top layer of chicken mixture with crushed corn chips (nacho cheese work well). Cover with foil and bake at 350° F for about 80 minutes. Remove foil for final ten minutes so chips on top are crispy.

Serve with chips, salsa, and a green salad dressed with a mixture of sour cream and salsa and topped with pepitas.

Carolyn Rose, author of *Hemlock Lake* and co-author of *The Big Grabowski*.
www.krillbooks.com

Egged Asparagus Casserole

Ingredients:

2 cans Jolly Green Giant asparagus (tender and cut)
1 can cream of mushroom soup
5 boiled eggs, sliced
American cheese slices (may substitute Velveeta, thinly sliced)
Cheese crackers, coarsely crumbled

Drain one can of asparagus and place in baking dish. Layer eggs, cheese, soup. Repeat. Top with cheese crackers. Bake at 400° F until brown and bubbly.

Susan Whitfield, author of the award-winning Logan Hunter Mystery series: *Genesis Beach, Just North of Luck, Hell Swamp, and Sin Creek.*
www.susanwhitfieldonline.com
www.susanwhitfield.blogspot.com
www.twitter.com/swhitfield

Grated Seafood Casserole

Ingredients:

1 lb pre-cooked shrimp
1 lb pre-cooked crabmeat (may use imitation)
2 cups cooked rice

Sauce:

1 stick melted butter
1 Tbsp flour
1 cup milk
1 ½ cups grated sharp cheddar cheese
1 tsp salt
Dash of black pepper
1 Tbsp Worcestershire Sauce
½ cup minced onion
1 tsp garlic, minced

Butter casserole dish. Place ½ of rice, ½ shrimp, and ½ crabmeat, and ½ sauce in that order. Repeat. Cover with cheese and bake at 350° F until bubbly.

Susan Whitfield, author of the award-winning Logan Hunter Mystery Series: *Genesis Beach, Just North of Luck, Hell Swamp, and Sin Creek.*
www.susanwhitfieldonline.com
www.susanwhitfield.blogspot.com
www.twitter.com/swhitfield

Hot Tamale Pie

Ingredients:

1 tsp salt
2 ½ cups boiling water
1 cup yellow cornmeal
½ cup cold water
2 Tbsp cooking oil
1 pound ground beef
1 medium onion, chopped
½ green pepper, chopped
1 cup green tomatoes, chopped & drained
2 mild chili peppers, chopped
1 cup ripe tomatoes, fresh or canned
1 tsp ground cumin seed
Chili powder to taste
Salt & pepper to taste

Add salt to boiling water. Slowly add cornmeal, which has been mixed with cold water. Cook 15 minutes over low heat, stirring frequently.

Meanwhile, sauté ground beef, onion, and green pepper in skillet until meat loses its red color. Add green tomato cubes and chili peppers and fry, stirring frequently, until lightly browned. Add ripe tomatoes, cumin, chili powder, salt and pepper. Simmer 10 minutes.

Alternate layers of cooked cornmeal and meat mixture into a well-greased casserole. Bake 30 minutes in a 350° F oven. Serves 4 to 6.

H. L. Chandler author of *The Keepers*.
www.hlchandler.bravehost.com

Jail House Asparagus or Broccoli Casserole

Preheat oven to 350° F

Ingredients:

2 pkg frozen asparagus or chopped broccoli (slightly thawed to workable)
1 cup grated sharp cheddar cheese
½ cup milk
1 can cream of mushroom soup
¾ cup saltine cracker crumbs
¼ tsp paprika
¼ cup slivered almonds
1 tsp Worcestershire sauce

Butter large casserole dish.
Layer cracker crumbs, vegetable, cheese (3 layers).
Heat soup, milk, and seasonings in saucepan until just about to boil and pour over casserole.
Top with almonds
Bake at 350° F for 45 minutes.

Harol Marshall, author of *Holy Death* and *A Corpse for Cuamantla*.
www.harolmarshall.com

Mountain Center Diner's French Fry Casserole

From the author's Youngblood series

Ingredients:

1 - 16 oz pagckage frozen Ore-Ida Golden Crinkles French Fries
¼ cup butter or margarine, melted
1 cup cheddar cheese, shredded
1 1/3 cups milk
3 whole eggs
1 ¼ tsp seasoned salt
¼ tsp onion powder

Preheat oven to 400° F. Toss golden crinkles with melted butter in a 1 ½ quart shallow baking dish or a 9" quiche pan.

Bake crinkles for 15 minutes. Remove from oven. Reduce heat to 350° F. Toss potatoes with cheese in casserole dish.

Beat together milk, eggs, and seasonings. Pour milk mixture over potatoes. Bake at 350° F for 20 to 25 minutes until knife in center comes out clean. Cool 5 minutes before cutting.

Keith Donnelly, author of the Donald Youngblood Mystery series: *Three Deuces Down* and *Three Days Dead*.
www.donaldyoungbloodmysteries.com

Mystery Surprise-Spaghetti Casserole

Made with leftover spaghetti and sauce

Ingredients:

8 oz spaghetti noodles, cooked
8 oz cream cheese
8 oz sour cream
8 oz mozzarella cheese, grated
1 lb ground meat, cooked and drained
26 oz spaghetti sauce
8 oz cheddar cheese, grated

Put noodles in bottom of 13" x 9" pan. Mix cream cheese and sour cream together, and spread on top of noodles. Spread other ingredients on in order listed. Bake at 350° F for 30 minutes.

The mystery is who submitted this recipe. All attempts failed to find her!

Perverted Pineapple Casserole

Ingredients:

20 oz can pineapple chunks
½ cup sugar
½ cup margarine
1 cup grated cheddar cheese (mild preferred)
3 Tbsp flour
1 cup Ritz cracker crumbs (broken up, not crushed)

Drain pineapple juice, reserving 3 Tbsp.
Combine flour, sugar, and juice.
Add cheese and pineapple.
Melt margarine and stir in crumbs, then spoon on top of mixture.
Bake at 350° F for 25 minutes.

Christy Tillery French, award-winning author of *The Bodyguard and the Snitch and Chasing Secrets.*
http://christytilleryfrench.com
http://damesofdialogue.wordpress.com

Speared Broccoli Casserole

Ingredients:

2 pkg frozen broccoli
1 egg, beaten
1 ½ cups grated cheddar, sharp
1 can cream of mushroom soup
1 cup mayonnaise
Cheese crackers, crumbled
1 medium onion, chopped

Cook broccoli in salt water until half done (should still be pretty firm). Drain and place in baking dish. Mix other ingredients and pour over broccoli. Add crackers. Bake uncovered at 350° F for 30 to 45 minutes or until brown and bubbly.

Susan Whitfield, author of the award-winning Logan Hunter Mystery series: *Genesis Beach, Just North of Luck, Hell Swamp, and Sin Creek.*
www.susanwhitfieldonline.com
www.susanwhitfield.blogspot.com
www.twitter.com/swhitfield

Spice-A-Roni

Preheat oven to 350° F

Ingredients:

2 to 3 cups cooked pasta, drained
1 can cream of mushroom soup
1 can Ro*Tel tomatoes, original
Cheese—cut up Velveeta or regular chunk cheese, 8 oz pkg pre-shredded cheese (save some for topping)
Dash of salt and pepper

Mix all ingredients together and pour into buttered casserole dish.
Top generously with shredded cheese of your choice.
Bake 30 minutes or until cheese topping is crusty or melted.
Add a dash of Tabasco sauce if you dare. Spice-A-Roni freezes beautifully.

Pat Browning, author of *Absinthe of Malice.*
www.pbrowning.blogspot.com
www.muderousmusings.blogspot.com

Suck-ulent Main Dishes

KATE'S WORKING MOM PIZZA

Asian Pork Bites

Ingredients:

1 - 16 oz package Fusili pasta
½ lb lean pork tenderloin, cut into bite size pieces
1 Tbsp olive oil
½ cup Sesame Ginger marinade (Lawry's)
½ - 16 oz package frozen broccoli florets
2 cups baby carrots, cut in quarters lengthwise
1 large onion cut in large chunks
1 Tbsp sesame seeds

Dressing:
½ cup pasta water
¼ cup honey
2 Tbsp soy sauce

Cook pasta in a large pot with plenty of water for 8 minutes. Drain, reserving ½ cup of the water for the dressing. In a large skillet, heat olive oil over medium heat. Add pork and cook 4 minutes. Add marinade, broccoli, carrots, and onion chunks and continue to cook for another 2 minutes or until vegetables are crisp tender. Meanwhile whisk together the dressing ingredients and set aside. In a large bowl, combine pasta and pork mixture. Drizzle with dressing and top with sesame seeds. Toss lightly before serving.

Caitlyn Hunter, author of *The Secret Life of Alice Smitty* in an L&L Dreamspell anthology.
http://caitlynhunter.com

Audacious Shrimp Scampi

Ingredients:

1 lb Linguine
1 ½ lb jumbo shrimp, shelled and deveined
Kosher salt and freshly ground black pepper
2 Tbsp extra virgin olive oil
2 tsp minced garlic
¼ cup Chardonnay
1 Tbsp freshly squeezed lemon juice
2 tsp finely chopped parsley

Boil 1 lb of Linguine until it becomes al dente. Drain and divide the pasta among 4 plates.

Put the shrimp on a large pie pan or plate and pat them dry with a paper towel. Arrange the shrimp so they lay flat.

Heat a large skillet over medium heat. Season the shrimp with salt and pepper. Add the Chardonnay, olive oil and garlic to the skillet. Invert the plate of shrimp over the pan so the shrimp fall into the pan all at once. Cook the shrimp, without moving them, for 1 minute. Turn the shrimp over and cook for 2 minutes more.

Divide the shrimp among 4 plates of Linguine, garnish with parsley and serve.

Amy Grech, author of *The Art of Deception* and *Blanket of White* and numerous stories.
www.crimsonscreams.com
http://twitter.com/amy_grech

Brazen New Mexico Salmon

Douse 1 lb salmon with lemon juice and let sit a few minutes.

Sprinkle with:
1 clove garlic, chopped
1 Jalapeno, fresh or canned, seeded and chopped
1 green onion, finely chopped
Onion powder
Garlic powder
More lemon juice
Olive oil
Cilantro, fresh and chopped

Bake 10 minutes in foil-lined pan at 500° F (or 10 minutes per inch of thickest part of fish). Switch oven to broil for 2 minutes.

Penny Rudolph, award-winning author of *Thicker Than Blood, Lifeblood, Eye of the Mountain God, and Listen to the Mockingbird.* www.pennyruddolph.com

Breaded Pork Chops

Heat oven to 400° F. Put nonstick aluminum foil on baking sheet (less calories), or melt 2 Tbsp butter to brush on the sheet.

Dry Mix:

1 ½ cups Bisquick
1 tsp salt
½ tsp cayenne pepper
1 tsp ground mustard

Wet Mix:

2 eggs
2 Tbsp milk

Dip chops in wet mix, then coat with dry mix. Place in a single layer on the baking sheet. Drizzle 2 Tbsp butter (real or light margarine) over the pork, or, to make them low-calorie, spray the chops with a thorough dousing of a butter-flavored cooking spray. Bake for 15 minutes. Turn the chops. If you didn't already put butter directly on the baking sheet, which should have already allowed that side of the chop to be browned, drizzle 2 Tbsp butter over the unbrowned side of the pork now or spray Pam on this side. Bake another 15 minutes, until nicely browned and crispy. DO NOT OVERCOOK. Test one chop for pinkness. Serve immediately.

Karen Wiesner, author of *First Draft in 30 Days* and From *First Draft to Finished Novel* (A Writer's Guide to Cohesive Story Building), Denim Blues Mysteries, and the Falcon's Bend series, co-authored with Chris Spindler.
http://www.karenwiesner.com
http://www.firstdraftin30days.com
http://www.falconsbend.com
http://www.JewelsoftheQuill.com

Burglar's Lasagna

Ingredients:

1 pkg lasagna noodles
1 ½ lbs hamburger meat
8 oz softened cream cheese
8 oz grated mozzarella cheese
8 oz grated cheese
1 lg jar spaghetti sauce
8 oz sour cream

Cook noodles according to package. Brown hamburger and add sauce to meat. Place noodles on bottom of the pan, ½ of sauce/meat mixture on top, ½ of sour cream & cream cheese placed by spoonfuls followed by ½ grated cheese. Repeat. Bake at 400° F for about 25 minutes until bubbly hot and cheese is melted.

Anne Patrick (Kinzie Monroe), author of 'Sweet' Edge of Your Seat Suspense: *Every Skull Tells A Story, Journey to Redemption, Lethal Dreams, Ties That Bind, Out of the Darkness,* and *Fire and Ash.*
http://www.suspensebyanne.blogspot.com/
http://www.kinziemonroe.blogspot.com/

Coo-Coo Coq au Vin

Coq au Vin is basically a chicken stew. The "Coq" in its name does not mean "chicken" but rather "rooster." Today we use chicken pieces. It tastes even better the day after it's made.

Step 1: Marinade Chicken Thighs
1 cup red wine (Tin Cup Merlot or a Beaujolais works well)
1 Tbsp vegetable oil
2 cloves garlic, crushed
2 bay leaves
3 whole cloves
Salt and pepper
1/3 cup onion, chopped fine
3 lbs chicken thighs (2 packages (about 10 pieces), frozen, skinned)

Mix first seven ingredients in a large bowl. Add skinned thighs. Cover and refrigerate for at least 18 hours. Longer is better. Strain off the red wine marinade, and save it. Discard bay leaves and onion bits.

Step 2: Prepare Vegetables and Broth
2 slices low-sodium bacon
1 parsnip, cut into small chunks
¾ cup carrots, cut into chunks
1/3 cup flour
2 ½ cups low-sodium chicken stock
1 small can tomato juice (6 oz)
2 sprigs of fresh thyme (or ¼ teaspoon dried thyme leaves)
2 onions, sliced the long way (or 25 pearl onions)

If using pearl onions, cut an X into them at the top before peeling, and drop them (with peels on) into boiling water for two minutes. Remove, discard water, and let onions cool. When cool, the peels will slip off. Set aside. If using regular onions, use half in next step and save remainder for last step.

Cook bacon in a deep skillet until crisp and crumbly. Remove bacon and set aside. Place carrots, parsnip, and first portion of sliced onion into skillet and sauté until onion is golden. Add 2 Tbsp of flour (save the rest) and stir to coat vegetables. Cook floured mixture 5 minutes, stirring often. Slowly add stock and then tomato juice to pan. Add fresh thyme. Simmer 30 minutes. Cool and strain to remove vegetables and thyme sprigs. Set aside.

Step 3: Brown chicken and mushrooms
3 Tbsp vegetable oil
Reserved flour
1 package button mushrooms (8 oz)

Dry the marinated chicken thighs with paper towels. Dredge chicken pieces in flour until coated lightly.

Heat oil in a clean skillet. Place chicken pieces in hot oil and cook until golden, not deeply browned. Do this in small batches to keep the oil evenly hot. Remove chicken pieces. Save oil and bits of chicken and flour in pan. Brush or wash mushrooms to remove grit. Peel mushrooms, saving stems. Cut tops and stems into rough quarters. Add to hot oil and cook until browned. Remove.

Step 4: Combine and bake
Chicken pieces
Reserved vegetable broth
Reserved red wine marinade
Reserved onion, bacon, and mushrooms

Preheat oven to 350° F.

Place browned chicken in an ovenproof pan. Strain the vegetables out of the broth. Pour the broth over the chicken. Add the reserved red wine marinade. Scrape bits from pan with mushrooms, and add to chicken. Place reserved sliced onion (or peeled pearl onions), crumbled bacon, and mushrooms around chicken pieces. Bake for 1½ hours or until chicken is tender.

Traditionally served over egg noodles, with salad and crusty bread. Serves 4 to 6.

Cash Anthony, author of *Yes, She Bites, A Bona Fide Quirk in the Law, and The Stand-In* from L&L Dreamspell's anthologies, and numerous short films and screenplays. www.lldreamspell.com

Chopped Picadillo

Ingredients:

1 lb ground beef
1 lb ground pork
2 large onions, chopped
1 green pepper, chopped
6 cloves of garlic, minced
Olive oil
6 tomatoes, chopped
2 tsp salt
Pepper
1 Tbsp brown sugar
¼ cup vinegar
¼ cup stuffed green olives, chopped
1 Tbsp capers
½ cup raisins (optional)
½ cup red wine

Sauté onions, peppers, and garlic in olive oil. When cooked, remove and sauté meat. Return cooked vegetables to pan and add remaining ingredients. Cook on low heat for about an hour. Add hot sauce to taste. Traditionally served over white rice. Freezes well.

Vicki Lane, author of the Elizabeth Goodweather Mystery series: *Old Wounds, Art's Blood, Signs in the Blood,* and *In a Dark Season.* www.vickilane.com

Cop-a-Plea Pork Roast

Ingredients:
1 – 3 to 4 pound pork roast
½ jar marmalade
1 jar maraschino cherries, undrained
3 cups petite carrots
2 large sweet potatoes
4 packets pork gravy
1 cup water
1 tsp salt
1 tsp pepper

Place pork roast in crock-pot. Peel and chop sweet potatoes and add to crock pot, along with carrots. Mix marmalade, maraschino cherries, gravy, water, salt, and pepper, and pour over roast. Cover and cook in crock-pot on low for 8 to 10 hours. Serves 4 to 6.

Cindy Keen Reynders, author of *The Saucy Lucy Murders* and *Paws-itively Guilty.*
www.cindykeenreynders.com

Crabby Jambalaya

Ingredients:

Olive or other cooking oil
1 medium onion, chopped
1 medium bell pepper, chopped
1 – 20 oz can (more or less) tomatoes *
Handful of sliced okra; fresh or frozen
Rice: Uncle Ben's brown/wild rice mix or frozen Birds Eye Steamfresh
2 to 4 cups chicken broth, depending on how soupy you like it
Shrimp (fresh or frozen, preferably with tails on) and, if desired,
pieces of ham; chunks of chicken; crab meat

* I use 2 10-oz cans of Ro*Tel Chunky Tomatoes and Green Chilies. They're so hot they make my eyes water but that takes care of spices. If you use regular chopped or crushed tomatoes you may want to add the optional spices listed below:
1 clove garlic, minced
1 small can mild green chilies
Dash of Tabasco sauce
Salt and pepper to taste

In heavy skillet or saucepan, sauté onion, bell pepper, and garlic in oil until tender, 5 to 10 minutes. Add tomatoes and chicken broth and cook about 10 minutes. Cover and leave it on. Warm for half an hour or so. Taste for seasoning. When ready to eat, add shrimp/crab/baked ham/chicken—any or all of them—just to heat through. Shrimp gets tough in a hurry. The minute it curls up it's done. Add shrimp, crab/ham/chicken when ready to serve. Cook rice according to directions. Put a heap of cooked rice on your plate and ladle jambalaya over it.

Pat Browning, author of *Absinthe Of Malice.*
www.authorsden.com/patbrowning
http://murderousmusings.blogspot.com
http://pbrowning.blogspot.com

Dangerous Diner's Chili

Ingredients:

1 lb ground beef
1 lb can kidney beans
12 oz bottle chili sauce
¼ tsp hot pepper sauce
½ tsp chili powder
2 Tbsp onion, chopped
1 tsp garlic salt
½ tsp Worcestershire sauce

Brown ground beef in pan. Drain off fat.
Stir in kidney beans plus liquid, and remaining ingredients.
Heat thoroughly.

Susanne Marie Knight, author of *The Wakefield Disturbance*.
www.susanneknight.com
www.unicalpress.com

Daring Shepherd's Lentil Pie

Ingredients:

½ lb dried lentils
1 can beef broth
1 onion chopped
1 carrot shredded
2 cloves garlic finely chopped
½ tsp salt
Pepper to taste
4 medium potatoes
2 Tbsp sour cream
1 tsp parsley

Cook lentils in water and beef broth until soft. Drain and either mash with a potato masher or with a hand held mixer. Sauté onions, garlic, and carrot in just a bit of cooking oil. Add to the lentils. Mix in salt and pepper to taste. Put this mix in a casserole dish—leave room for potato topping.
Boil and mash potatoes. Add the sour cream and parsley. Smooth this on top of the lentils. Cover the casserole with a lid and bake in a 350° F oven for ½ hour until flavors blend.
Serves 4 to 6.
Raven Bower, author of *Apparitions*.
www.ravenbower.com

Demon-Fire Burritos

Ingredients:

Pork roast (shoulder is fine)
Flour tortillas
Monterey Jack cheese, shredded
1 - 12 oz can Stagg Chili (or similar spicy chili)
1 - 12 oz can refried beans
1 - 12 oz can diced potatoes
Nacho-sliced jalapenos to taste

Place roast in crock pot (fat layer up) and cover with combination water and jalapeno juice. Cook on high for 12 hours while maintaining water level. (Roast should fall apart when finished.) Remove any fat or bones and shred cooked pork.
In a pot, mix chili, refried beans, shredded cheese, diced potatoes, and jalapenos (to taste).
Spoon mixture onto tortilla end and add pork. Roll and enjoy.

Tim Marquitz, author of *Sepulchral Earth*.
www.tmarquitz.com

Evil Gazpacho

Ingredients:

1 slice whole wheat bread, torn in very small pieces
5 large ripe tomatoes chopped
2 medium cucumbers, peeled and chopped
1 medium green pepper chopped
1 medium sweet onion chopped
1 cup water
¼ cup olive oil
½ cup red wine vinegar
2 large cloves garlic finely chopped
1 tsp sea salt
3 to 5 fresh basil leaves torn in small pieces
1/8 tsp pepper
Juice of one fresh, medium-sized lime, plus zest from lime

Mix bread, ¾ of the chopped tomatoes, one chopped cucumber, one quarter green pepper, one half onion, the water and oil in a large bowl.
Blend the remaining ingredients in a blender until they become a thick liquid. Pour contents of blender into the bowl with the other ingredients, stir together, and chill. Serve cold. Garnish with fresh parsley if desired.

L.C. Evans, author of *Talented Horsewoman, Jobless Recovery, Night Camp,* and *We Interrupt This Date.*
http://lcevans.com

Filleted Catfish in the Manner of Vera Cruz

Ingredients:

20 large shrimp, raw, peeled
4 large filets of catfish
Plain Yogurt (about two cups)
Guajillo sauce or Dijon Mustard (about two Tbsp)
Flour
Konriko seasoned salt
Canola oil
1 green pepper, chopped
1 large onion, chopped
3 to 5 cloves of garlic, chopped
2 to 3 tomatoes, chopped
1 to 2 jalapeno peppers, chopped
1 cup small stuffed Spanish olives
Salsa (optional)
Olive oil
Cilantro (optional)

Put the shrimp on skewers. They will be grilled to provide a garnish for the fried fish.

Mix the yogurt and mustard or guajillo sauce and put the catfish filets in it to marinate while you make the salsa.

Sauté all the chopped vegetables in a little olive oil. Add tomatoes after the others have wilted. When the tomatoes have cooked down a bit, add a bit of store-bought salsa if you feel like it, and the olives. Don't cook the olives too much. Put some flour on a plate and add the seasoned salt. Roll the yogurt soaked fish in the flour. Fry in canola oil.

To serve, top each filet with five grilled shrimp, pour the heated salsa over, finish with chopped cilantro, if you like it. Serves four.

Vicki Lane, author of the Elizabeth Goodweather Mystery series: *Old Wounds, Art's Blood, Signs in the Blood*, and *In A Dark Season*. www.vickilane.com

Gabe's Jailhouse Ribs

Ingredients:

4 lbs country-style spare ribs
½ cup water
1 small onion
½ cup brown sugar
1 ¼ cups ketchup
1 bottle hickory smoke flavored barbecue sauce

Combine water, chopped onion, brown sugar, ketchup and barbecue sauce. Brush sauce on ribs and pour into 5-quart crockpot. Cover and cook 8 to 10 hours on low. Serves 4 to 6.
Cindy Keen Reynders, author of The Saucy Lucy Mysteries and *Paws-itively Guilty*.
www.cindykeenreynders.com

Guilty Greek Shrimp

Ingredients:

1 lb shelled, deveined medium shrimp
2 large sweet onions, peeled and quartered
2 cans (14.5 oz) stewed tomatoes
1/3 cup olive oil
½ cup dry white wine
½ Tbsp cumin
Salt and pepper to taste
3 Tbsp olive oil
½ tsp garlic powder
½ cup heavy cream
1 - 4 oz pkg crumbled feta cheese
½ cup ouzo

Heat 1/3 cup olive oil in 12-inch, heavy skillet. While oil is heating, chop onions very fine in a food processor. Pour onions into hot oil. Cook on medium heat, stirring occasionally. While onions are cooking, spread out shrimp on paper towels to drain. Drain stewed tomatoes and rinse. Puree tomatoes in the food processor. When onions are limp and transparent, add tomatoes and bring mixture to a boil. Add white wine and turn heat down to a gentle simmer. Add cumin, salt, & pepper to taste. Cover, and simmer mixture on low heat, stirring occasionally, for at least 30 minutes, until sauce has thickened. Meanwhile, heat 3 Tbsp olive oil in small, 8 inch frying pan on medium heat. Sprinkle garlic powder into the olive oil. Pat shrimp dry. Place shrimp into frying pan in single layer. Sauté on one side, then turn and sauté on the other side until pink. Lift the shrimp out using a slotted spoon, and place in small individual baking dishes.

Place a single layer of the remaining shrimp into the frying pan. Sauté as above. Repeat until all shrimp have been prepared. Arrange them to fill four individual baking dishes.

Once tomato and onion mixture has thickened, remove cover and add heavy cream. Stir until cream is mixed throughout the sauce and turn off heat. Spoon sauce over shrimp in four baking dishes. Pour ouzo into small saucepan. Heat on medium heat until steaming. Remove from heat. Light a wooden match and set hot ouzo aflame in saucepan. Let the flames burn out, then pour ouzo as evenly as possible over contents of each individual baking dish. Sprinkle crumbled feta cheese over each baking dish, to cover the sauce topping the shrimp. Bake at 375° F in heated oven for ½ hour. Serve with bread and salad.

Elaine Marie Alphin, author of *Counterfeit Son* (Winner of the Edgar Award), *Ghost Soldier, Perfect Shot Picture Perfect* and *An Unspeakable Crime: The Prosecution and Persecution of Leo Frank.*
http://www.elainemariealphin.com
http://elainealphin.blogspot.com

Intense Cincinnati-Style Chili

As featured in *Caviar Dreams*

Ingredients:

2 lbs lean ground beef
2 tsp crushed red pepper
4 small onions, chopped
1 quart water
2 Tbsp Worcestershire sauce
1 tsp salt
1 tsp garlic powder
1½ Tbsp vinegar
4 tsp chili powder
1 tsp ground allspice
6 oz tomato paste
5 medium bay leaves
1 block unsweetened chocolate (yes, people in Cincinnati like chocolate in their chili)
4 tsp cumin

Add ground beef to water in a large pot and stir until beef separates to a fine texture. Add all other ingredients. Stir to blend. Bring to a boil and reduce heat to simmer uncovered for about 3 hours. May cover for the last hour if desired consistency has been reached. For the classic Three Way, serve on spaghetti with shredded cheese. For a Four Way, add onions. If you're really brave for a Five Way, add the beans. And don't forget the hot sauce and oyster crackers.

Judy Nichols, author of *Caviar Dreams*.
www.judy5cents.com

Kate's Working Mom Pizza

As featured in *Tree Huggers*

Ingredients:

Ready made pizza crust
Shredded mozzarella cheese (as much as you want)
1 jar pasta sauce
Fresh Spinach
Imitation crabmeat
Chopped mushrooms (optional)
Green olives (optional) or toppings of choice
Olive oil

Preheat oven to 450° F. Spread the sauce on the pizza, cover with shredded cheese. Then cover entire pizza with fresh spinach, followed by imitation crabmeat. Cover half the pizza with chopped mushrooms and the other half with green olives. Drizzle with olive oil. Make sure to let the kids help.

Turn oven down to 425° F and place pizza on middle rack. Bake for 7½ to 10 minutes, or until done.

Judy Nichols, author of *Tree Huggers*.
www.judy5cents.com

Maced Moussaka

Vegetable Base: Tofu "Béchamel" Sauce:
3 large eggplants
1 package silken tofu (can use light)
Salt
½ cup cottage cheese (can use reduced fat)
¼ to ½ cup extra virgin olive oil
¼ cup non fat milk
Dash of nutmeg

Meat Sauce:
Dash of mace
4 Tbsp butter
3 cups chopped onion
2 cloves garlic, finely minced
1 lb lean ground lamb
1 lb lean ground beef

Tomato Sauce:
2 cups Tomato Sauce (see below)
1 onion, chopped
2 bay leaves
1 Tbsp olive oil
Pinch of dried oregano
1 small can tomato paste
Freshly ground black pepper
2 cups beef stock
2 cups dry red wine
2 fresh tomatoes, chopped
½ tsp ground cinnamon
¼ tsp fresh thyme
2 Tbsp chopped fresh parsley
Salt and pepper to taste
10 fresh mushrooms
1 cup freshly grated Romano or Parmesan cheese

Prepare the meat sauce:
Melt 3 Tbsp butter over low heat in large deep pan, reserving 1 Tbsp for cooking mushrooms later. Add chopped onions and garlic, and cook until golden. Add ground meats and cook over medium high heat until browned. Break up any large lumps. Use a crumpled paper towel to wipe out sides and bottom of the skillet. Set aside.

Prepare the tomato sauce:
Place the items for the tomato sauce together. Chop the onion. Place in a medium-sized saucepan and cook in olive oil until translucent. Add the tomato paste and cook, stirring to blend. Add the stock, fresh tomatoes, and thyme. Simmer 45 minutes, then blend or process until smooth. A Smart Stick works well for this.

Mix meat sauce, tomato sauce, wine, and spices:
When the tomato sauce is ready, add it and the bay leaves, oregano, black pepper, red wine, cinnamon, and parsley to the meat in the deep pan. Add salt and pepper to taste, and cook over very low heat until most liquid is absorbed. This may take an hour. Stir often, and watch closely at the end to avoid scorching.

Prepare the eggplant:
Rinse the eggplants off. Cut off the stem ends and the bottoms, and slice them into ¼-inch rounds. Place the slices on a double-thickness of paper towels, spread out on a counter or on a tray. Sprinkle the rounds heavily with salt, and cover with another thickness of paper towel. Over as much of the eggplant slices as possible, place pie plates or dinner plates, gently pressing the rounds to squeeze the excess water from them. (This will remove the bitterness.) Let stand for 45 minutes, then rinse, and drain. Dry the slices on paper towels.

Heat the oven to 400° F.

Line several baking sheets or trays with aluminum foil. Using a pastry brush, brush each eggplant round lightly with olive oil. Turn the rounds over and repeat, placing the oiled rounds on the aluminum foil. Bake the eggplant rounds until lightly browned on one side, about 10 minutes.

Prepare the mushrooms:
Trim and peel the mushrooms. Slice into thin pieces, and sauté in the reserved 1 Tbsp of butter. Add the sautéed mushrooms to the meat mixture.

Make the Tofu Béchamel Sauce:
Place the whole package of silken tofu in a blender. Add the cottage cheese. Blend for three minutes, minimum. When the mixture begins to look smooth, add the non fat milk to get a creamier consistency. Add the nutmeg and mace. Taste and adjust texture or seasonings. This will taste a little "beany" but it will pass for a cream sauce with far fewer calories.

Assemble the Moussaka:
Spray a large baking tray or roasting pan with Pam. Place half the eggplant slices in the bottom in one layer—overlapping if necessary. Add the meat mixture. Top with remaining eggplant rounds. Pour the Tofu Béchamel Sauce over the top layer and sprinkle with the grated cheese.

Bake for 45 minutes to one hour at 400° F, until golden brown. Let stand at least 30 minutes.

Cash Anthony, author of *A Bona Fide Quirk in the Law, The Best Man* and *The Stand-In* from L&L Dreamspell's anthologies, and numerous short films and screenplays.
www.lldreamspell.com

Mary's Country-Style Backbones

Mary is a character in the author's mystery series

Choose pork backbones that are thick, lean, and meaty with bone in. Boil gently in just enough water to cover. Boil until tender, but not falling off the bone.

Arrange ribs in a shallow pan and baste with sauce.* Bake at 400° F for 15 minutes, turn and baste again, then continue baking for 15 minutes more. Place under broiler for a few minutes for added crispness.

You can also baste ribs and cook on outdoor grill until warmed through and crusty.

*Smoky BBQ Sauce:
½ cup ketchup
½ cup chili sauce
1/3 cup honey
Colgin Liquid Smoke hickory smoke flavoring to taste

Cook's tip: To make a quart of sauce, mix a 12 oz bottle of ketchup, a 12 oz bottle of chili sauce and an 8 oz bottle of honey. Add Liquid Smoke to taste. Keep refrigerated.

Keith Donnelly, author of the Donald Youngblood Mystery series: *Three Deuces Down* and *Three Days Dead.*
www.donaldyoungbloodmysteries.com

Mystery Meatloaf

For a quality meatloaf that's low in cholesterol and fat, start with one pound of 93% fat free ground beef.

Add the following to the meat:
½ cup of quick oats
2 Tbsp ground flaxseed
2 Tbsp ketchup
1 Tbsp yellow mustard
½ tsp salt
½ tsp ginger
1 tsp cilantro

Mix this altogether and shape into a meatloaf.
Place in open baking pan and bake at 350° F. After half an hour, turn meatloaf over with a spatula. Pour tomato sauce over loaf.

Bake for another 30 minutes or 20 if you prefer less well done.

While you are baking your meatloaf, throw potatoes and yams in the oven to bake. You should actually start your potatoes before the meatloaf so that they will be done.

Toss a salad or steam a vegetable and you have a hearty and nutritious dinner for two.

Jacqueline Seewald, author of *The Drowning Pool* and *The Inferno Collection*.
www.jacquelineseewald.com

Nut Case Tilapia

Ingredients:

½ cup finely ground dry breadcrumbs
¼ cup finely chopped pecans
¼ tsp garlic powder
¼ tsp paprika
¼ tsp black pepper
½ cup low-fat buttermilk
½ tsp Cholula or equivalent hot sauce
3 Tbsp flour
4 (6 oz) tilapia fillets
1 Tbsp olive oil
4 lemon wedges

Combine first five ingredients in shallow dish.
Combine buttermilk and hot sauce in shallow dish.
Place flour in third shallow dish.
Dredge each fillet in flour, then buttermilk mixture, then bread-crumb/pecan mixture.
Heat ½ of the oil to just sizzling and add 2 fillets. Cook 2 to 3 minutes on each side (fish should flake easily with fork). Repeat for remaining fillets. Serves four. Serve with lemon wedges.

Harol Marshall, author of *Holy Death* and *A Corpse for Cuamantla*.
www.harolmarshall.com

On The Lamb Chops

Ingredients:

Garlic, minced
Rosemary, roughly chopped
Olive oil
Lamb chops

Mix together chopped garlic, rosemary, and olive oil.
Put lamb chops into mixture and turn. Leave in refrigerator overnight.
Heat a skillet on high.
Put lamb chops in skillet and sear about 3 minutes per side (more for more well done).

Mark Rosendorf, author of *The Rasner Effect* and *Without Hesitation: The Rasner Effect II*.
www.markrosendorf.com

Pepperoncini Roast

Ingredients:

1 beef or pork roast of your choice—trim off all fat
1 - 16 oz jar pepperoncini (your choice of strength)
Swiss cheese
Rolls

Place well trimmed roast in crock-pot. Pour jar of pepperoncini over meat. Let cook until roast is easily pulled apart with a fork. Serve on rolls with slices of Swiss cheese.
Can also be used as a main dish without making a sandwich.

Lynette Hall Hampton, author of *Stetson Mold*, and the Reverend Willa Hinshaw series.
www.lynettehallahampton.com

Radical Meatloaf

Ingredients:

3 lbs hamburger meat
1 sleeve of Ritz Crackers
1 egg
¾ cup Heinz Ketchup
1 medium sweet onion, chopped
Salt
Pepper
Lawry's Seasoning Salt

In a big bowl, mix hamburger meat, 1 sleeve of crackers, crushed, egg, chopped onion, 1 tsp salt, 1 tsp pepper, 1 tsp Lawry's Seasoning Salt, and ¾ cup of ketchup. Mix thoroughly.

Shape into loaf and place on greased broiler pan, cover the entire loaf with ketchup, and bake at 350° F for 1 to 1½ hours or until done.

Melinda Elmore, author of *Native Dreams.*
www.melindaelmore.webs.com
www.melindaelmoreauthorofmysteryromance.blogspot.com
www.melinda4.wordpress.com
www.melinda.essentialwriters.com

Ruthless Mediterranean Eggplant Lasagna

Ingredients:

2 large eggplants
16 oz container ricotta cheese (room temperature)
1 Tbsp dried basil
1 Tbsp dried oregano
4 oz package feta cheese
8 oz package shredded mozzarella cheese
2 Tbsp black pepper
1 Tbsp garlic powder
6 oz chopped frozen spinach (thawed)
1 package lasagna-shaped pasta, cooked
Pre-made tomato sauce (meatless)

Preheat your oven to 350° F. Spray baking sheet and baking dish with cooking spray. Peel the skin off eggplant and discard skin. Cut off the top of the eggplants, and then cut in half lengthwise. Lay each half of the eggplant flat side down on your cutting surface, and cut into thin 1/4-inch strips. Place each strip onto baking sheet, making sure not to overlap. Spray eggplant with cooking spray. Place in oven uncovered for 10 minutes. Note: If you have a small oven, you may need to do this in two batches.

Take eggplant out of oven. Raise oven temperature to 425° F. Empty container of ricotta cheese into mixing bowl. Sprinkle basil, oregano, feta cheese and half of mozzarella cheese on top. Drop spinach into mixture. Sprinkle pepper and garlic on top. Mix until all ingredients are combined.

Place lasagna pasta on the bottom of baking dish, making sure to cover the entire bottom. Place a layer of eggplant on top of that, covering entire layer of pasta. Top eggplant with ricotta cheese mixture. Top ricotta cheese with tomato sauce. Repeat this step two more times.

Place an additional layer of lasagna pasta on top of top layer of sauce. Place another layer of sauce on top of the pasta. Sprinkle with remaining mozzarella cheese. Cover baking dish with aluminum foil. Place in oven for one hour.

Take lasagna out of oven. Let cool, covered for 10 minutes. Uncover, cut into squares, and serve hot.

James Mascia, author of *High School Heroes*.
www.islandofdren.com

Sauced Shepherd's Pie

Ingredients:

1½ lb lean ground beef
2 Tbsp butter
1 tsp Worcestershire sauce
2 eggs, separated
6 Tbsp additional butter
8 potatoes, peeled, boiled, and mashed
1 cup finely chopped onion
½ cup chopped green pepper
1 Tbsp ketchup
6 or more Tbsp of beef broth
½ cup heavy cream
¼ tsp garlic powder
Parmesan cheese
Optional, hot sauce to taste

Brown ground beef and sauté onions and peppers in 2 Tbsp of butter until golden. Mix ground beef with onions, peppers, ketchup, Worcestershire sauce and optional hot sauce. Salt and pepper to taste. Add a few Tbsp of beef broth and cook, covered, over low heat for 15 to 20 minutes, adding more broth as necessary to keep moist. Beat egg yolks until light, then in another bowl, beat egg whites until stiff. Beat the yolks, cream, 6 Tbsp of butter and garlic powder into hot mashed potatoes. Gently fold in beaten egg whites. Put meat mixture into casserole then top with potato mixture. Sprinkle Parmesan cheese on top and bake at 350° F until potato topping is puffed and browned, about 25 to 35 minutes. Serves 8. (Recipe used with permission of Rosie McLean of Rosie's Home Cookin'.)

JD Webb, author of *Shepard's Pie, Moon Over Chicago, Her Name Is Mommy, Smudge.*
www.jdwebb.com

Saucy Lucy Spaghetti

Ingredients:

1 lb ground beef
1 lb Italian sausage
4 – 14 ½ oz cans of diced tomatoes, undrained
6 – 6 oz cans tomato paste
1 – 8 oz can of mushrooms
1 cup beef broth
¼ cup packed brown sugar
3 Tbsp dried Marjoram
2 Tbsp garlic powder
2 Tbsp onion powder
2 Tbsp dried basil leaves
2 Tbsp Italian seasoning
1 tsp salt
1 bay leaf
Hot cooked spaghetti noodles

Brown ground beef and sausage in large skillet over medium heat; drain. Mix meat, along with tomatoes, tomato paste, mushrooms, broth, brown sugar, and seasonings in a 5-quart crock-pot. Cover and cook on low for 5 to 8 hours or until bubbly. Discard bay leaf and serve sauce over spaghetti. Serves 12 to 14 or the sauce freezes well.

Cindy Keen Reynders, author of The Saucy Lucy Mysteries and *Paws-itively Guilty.*
www.cindykeenreynders.com

Schizophrenic Sweet and Sour Pork

Ingredients:

Sweet and Sour Sauce:
½ cup sugar
2 ½ Tbsp cornstarch
2 ½ tsp apple cider vinegar
1 cup water
2 Tbsp gluten-free soy sauce
3 Tbsp catsup

Stir all ingredients together in medium-sized pot. Bring to a slow boil. Turn off burner and set aside.

Sweet and Sour Pork:
1 lb pork cut into 1 inch cubes
1 onion, sliced
1 green pepper, cut into strips
20 oz can pineapple chunks

Batter:
1 cup white rice flour
2 tsp baking powder
½ tsp salt
2 eggs
½ cup milk
2 Tbsp vegetable oil
Oil for frying

Simmer pork in frying pan until cooked through. Prepare batter by combining flour, powder, and salt in a bowl. Combine eggs, milk, and oil in separate bowl. Stir dry ingredients and mix until smooth. Add pork to batter, coating each cube well. Fry battered pork in oil. In separate skillet, add just enough oil to cover the bottom. Cook onion for 3 minutes. Add peppers and cook for another minute. Add sweet and sour sauce to the vegetables. Cook uncovered for about 2 minutes. Add drained pineapple and simmer to keep warm. Pour pork over a bed of rice. With a ladle, pour sweet and sour sauce over pork and rice.

Michelle Hollstein-Matkins, author of The Aggie Underhill Mysteries.
www.MichelleAnnHollstein.com

Seedy Korean Beef

Ingredients:

2 lbs sirloin, stripped
Sesame seeds, crushed
2 tsp sugar
1 tsp onion salt
1 tsp garlic salt
1/3 cup soy sauce
½ tsp ginger
¼ tsp. Accent
Pepper
Swish of beer

Combine all ingredients and marinate four hours. Broil 2 minutes each side.

Susan Whitfield, author of the award-winning Logan Hunter Mystery series: *Genesis Beach, Just North of Luck, Hell Swamp, and Sin Creek.*
www.susanwhitfieldonline.com
www.susanwhitfield.blogspot.com
www.twitter.com/swhitfield

Shotgun Chili

Ingredients:

4 lbs ground venison (may substitute hamburger)
1 lg can tomato juice
1 lg onion, chopped
1 to 2 cans kidney beans, drained
1/3 cup brown sugar
Chili powder
Green, red, orange, yellow peppers, chopped, (may use Jalapenos for more heat)

Brown meat and drain. In large stockpot, put meat, onions, beans, and peppers. Add brown sugar and chili powder to taste. Simmer 1½ hours.

Susan Whitfield, author the award-winning Logan Hunter Mystery series: *Genesis Beach, Just North of Luck, Hell Swamp, and Sin Creek.*
www.susanwhitfieldonline.com
www.susanwhitfield.blogspot.com
www.twitter.com/swhitfield

Sin-sational Shrimp Pasta

Ingredients:

1 serving angel hair pasta (or penne pasta, if a heartier meal is desired)
4 to 6 cooked (frozen) medium shrimp
1 Tbsp butter
1 ½ tsp lemon juice
1 Tbsp freshly chopped dill (or 1 tsp dried dill)

Multiply ingredients by the number of people to be served. If serving more than 1, reduce the butter, lemon and dill by half.

Place frozen shrimp in cold water to thaw. Boil water and cook pasta according to package directions. During last minute of cooking time for pasta, add shrimp to water. When water returns to a boil, drain and toss pasta and shrimp with dill-seasoned lemon butter. Serve hot with tossed green salad and French or Italian bread toasted with "Sin-sational Spread":

½ cup butter (1/4 lb), softened
2 tsp sesame seeds
1 tsp garlic powder
½ tsp onion salt
1 Tbsp freshly chopped thyme (or 1 tsp dried thyme)
½ tsp black pepper

Mix all ingredients together until well blended—or melt the butter, remove from heat and mix in the remaining ingredients. Spread on sliced bread—or cut ½ loaf of French bread lengthwise and spread with seasoned butter. Heat under broiler until lightly toasted.

Suzanne Young, author of *Murder by Yew*.
www.suzanneyoungbooks.com

Skinned Chicken Piccata

Ingredients:

4 boneless, skinless chicken breasts sliced into chunks
¼ cup all-purpose flour
1 cup bread crumbs
1/8 teaspoon salt
1/8 teaspoon pepper
5 Tbsp butter
¼ cup white wine
¼ cup lemon juice
Half a box of ziti or spaghetti

In a dish, coat chicken chunks with bread crumbs. In a separate bowl, combine flour, salt, and pepper. Coat chicken with flour mixture. Shake off excess. Melt butter in a skillet. Add chicken and sauté over medium heat for 10 minutes or until cooked through, turning once. While chicken is sautéing, prepare pasta following directions on the box. Once chicken is cooked through, push chicken to one side of skillet and add wine and lemon juice. Boil for a couple of minutes. Add cooked pasta. Stir chicken and pasta until well coated in the sauce.

Stacy Juba, author of *Twenty-Five Years Ago Today; Sink or Swim; Face-Off* (under Stacy Drumtra).
www.stacyjuba.com

Tequila Chicken

Ingredients:

2 boneless/skinless chicken breasts pounded to about 3/4 inch thick

Marinate 30 to 60 min at room temp in:
¼ cup Italian Salad Dressing
¼ cup Tbsp Tequila
¼ tsp crushed Red Chile
1 tsp diced garlic

Dredge in flour and sauté in 2 tsp each olive oil and butter until golden brown.

Penny Rudolph, award-winning author of *Thicker Than Blood, Lifeblood, Eye of the Mountain God,* and *Listen to the Mockingbird.* www.pennyrudolph.com

Third-Degree Chicken Melt

Ingredients:

Boneless and skinless chicken breast
Lawry's Louisiana Red Pepper Marinade (or similar)
Bell peppers (red & green)
Fresh garlic
Monterey Jack cheese
Fresh jalapenos

Place thawed chicken breast inside a sealable freezer bag and pound flat (to about a ¼ inch thickness).
Place chicken breast in a dish and cover in marinade.
Let sit overnight (or longer if desired).

Dice bell peppers, garlic (to taste: one clove for 8 chicken breasts), and jalapenos together, and then grate cheese.

Spread marinated chicken breast on a baking sheet.

On half of the chicken breast, add a thick layer of grated cheese, and then spoon in vegetable mixture, covered with another layer of cheese.

Fold chicken breast in half and secure with a toothpick.

Cook at 350° F until chicken is a reddish-brown.

Tim Marquitz, author of *Sepulchral Earth*.
www.tmarquitz.com

Vicious Vegetarian Lasagna

Ingredients:

9 strips lasagna noodles, cooked
½ Jar Classico Mushrooms & Ripe Olives Pasta Sauce
1 green eggplant, peeled and sliced, raw
1 cup small broccoli heads, raw
1 pound beef or turkey burger, raw (optional ingredient for
meat eaters)
Shredded Mozzarella Cheese
½ cup water

Pour water into 8" x 8" glass casserole dish.
Cut lasagna noodles to fit casserole and lay in 1/3 of the noodles.
Add a layer each of raw eggplant slices and broccoli heads.
Add layer of burger.
Sprinkle with desired amount of Mozzarella cheese.
Cover with a layer of pasta sauce.
Add another layer of noodles and repeat layering of other ingredients.
Cover top with a layer of noodles. Cover completely with balance of pasta sauce.
Cover dish with aluminum foil and crimp to seal well.
Bake in 325° F oven for 1½ hours, until meat and vegetables are done, or cook in combo microwave/convection oven on High for 20 minutes or until done.
(Recipe ingredients should be doubled for 9" x 13" glass pan.)
Cooking time for larger dish is the same but 2 hours in regular oven, 30 minutes in Micro/Convection oven can't hurt recipe.

Mary Deal, author of *River Bones*.
www.WriteAnyGenre.com

Zombie's Roast Turkey

Ingredients:

1 turkey, fresh (or thawed)
1/8 cup salt for cleaning
½ rib celery
¼ medium onion
½ medium carrot

Rub:
1 tsp salt
1 tsp dried garlic
1 tsp sage
1 tsp thyme
½ tsp tarragon
½ tsp paprika
½ tsp pepper flakes
¼ tsp black pepper
¼ tsp celery seed

Preheat oven to 275° F. Remove giblets from turkey and rinse thoroughly with cold water. Put 1/8 cup of salt on wet hands and scour turkey inside and out. Rinse again.

While turkey is drying, combine rub ingredients and grind together until well blended. Rub inside turkey and under the breast skin. Put celery, onion, and carrot into the turkey cavity and place in a roaster with lid (or cover with foil). Bake until meat thermometer reads 190° F. Remove lid or foil and switch oven to broil for about 5 minutes, watching carefully and removing as soon as skin crisps. Let stand for 10-20 minutes before carving. Cavity vegetables can be blended into gravy.

T.L. Ryder, author of *No Place Like Home* (Under the Moon's Undead Embrace Anthology.)
www.underthemoon.org/undeadembrace.html

VICIOUS VEGETARIAN LASAGNA

Unlawful Vegetables

MURDER
BY POTATO

Bold Butternut Squash

Ingredients:

2 good-sized butternut squash, halved and seeded
Olive oil
1 lb bulk hot sausage
1 tart apple, chopped
Butter
1 cup Pepperidge Farm herb stuffing
Celery—5 or 6 stalks, chopped
2 medium onions, chopped
1 or 2 hot peppers, chopped (with or without seeds and ribs depending on how hot you like it)
3 or 4 calamondins (or kumquats), chopped, including peel
1 cup chopped pecans

Preheat oven to 375° F.
Lightly oil baking dish.
Half squash lengthwise and remove seeds.
Arrange squash cut side up on the baking dish.
Bake until almost tender, 30 to 40 minutes.
Keep the oven on.

Meanwhile, crumble the sausage into a skillet and cook over medium heat until no longer pink. Add apple. Cook, stirring until crisp-tender. Remove from pan and let cool slightly.

Sauté onion, celery, and hot pepper in butter until limp. Combine vegetables with sausage and apple; add stuffing, calamondins, pecans, and a little water or orange juice to moisten. Scoop out the squash, leaving 3/8 inch thick shells.

Lightly mix the squash pulp into the sausage mixture. Pile the stuffing into the squash halves. Bake uncovered until piping hot and brown and crusty on top, 20 to 25 minutes.

Let cool for several minutes before serving. This also works as a completely decadent stuffing for pork tenderloin.

Vicki Lane, author of The Elizabeth Goodweather Mystery Series: *Old Wounds, Art's Blood, Signs in the Blood, and In A Dark Season.* www.vickilane.com

Copious Cheesy Potatoes

Ingredients:

6 medium russet potatoes, peeled and thinly sliced
1 stick butter
¼ cup onion, diced
2 Tbsp white rice flour
1 tsp salt
Dash of pepper
2 cups milk
3 cups shredded mild cheddar cheese

Preheat oven to 350° F.

Spread potatoes in bottom of 9" x 13" baking pan. In a saucepan, melt butter and sauté onions. Add flour, salt, and pepper. Cook until the butter thickens. Add milk and 2 cups of cheese. Stir continuously until cheese sauce begins to boil around the edges. Pour sauce over potatoes. Bake one hour. Sprinkle remaining cheese over the top and bake for another 10 minutes until melted and browned.

Michelle Hollstein-Matkins, author of the Aggie Underhill Mystery series.
www.MichelleAnnHollstein.com

Cracked Eggplant Parmesan

Ingredients:

1 lg eggplant, peeled and cut into wheels
Salt
2 eggs, beaten
1 ½ cups cracker crumbs
2 cups shredded mozzarella
¼ cup Parmesan cheese
Your favorite tomato/meat sauce
Cooking oil

Sprinkle eggplant with salt and place in a bowl to "sweat". Drain after 30 minutes. Dip each wheel into egg and coat with crumbs. Fry in hot oil until brown. Drain on paper towels.
Place ½ of eggplant in greased dish. Layer with sauce and cheeses. Repeat. Bake at 350° F for 20 to 25 minutes.

Susan Whitfield, author of the award-winning Logan Hunter Mystery Series: *Genesis Beach, Just North of Luck, Hell Swamp, and Sin Creek.*
www.susanwhitfieldonline.com
www.susanwhitfield.blogspot.com
www.twitter.com/swhitfield

Drunken Baked Beans

Ingredients:

1 large can baked beans
½ cup bourbon
½ cup chili sauce
1 Tbsp brown sugar
¼ cup molasses
½ lb bacon, uncooked

Combine all ingredients and top with bacon. Bake at 350° F for 20 to 30 minutes.

Susan Whitfield, author of the award-winning Logan Hunter Mystery Series: *Genesis Beach, Just North of Luck, Hell Swamp, and Sin Creek.*
www.susanwhitfieldonline.com
www.susanwhitfield.blogspot.com
www.twitter.com/swhitfield

Electrocutioner's Zucchini Sticks

Ingredients:

¾ cup flour
1 tsp salt
¼ tsp garlic, minced or powder
Dash of pepper
3/4 cup milk
2 eggs, separated
2 Tbsp oil
3 medium zucchini, sliced into small sticks
Cooking oil

Combine flour, salt, garlic, and pepper. Add egg yolks, milk, and 2 Tbsp of oil. Batter may be lumpy. Beat egg whites until stiff. Gently fold into batter. Dip zucchini sticks in batter and deep fry until golden brown.

Susan Whitfield, author of the award-winning Logan Hunter Mystery Series; *Genesis Beach, Just North of Luck, Hell Swamp, and Sin Creek.*
www.susanwhitfieldonline.com
www.susanwhitfield.blogspot.com
www.twitter.com/swhitfield

Flamed Indiana Fried Cabbage

Ingredients:

3 Tbsp salted butter (margarine or olive oil will work, but butter gives it a better flavor)
½ medium onion, chopped
½ green pepper
½ cup of chopped carrots
½ small head of cabbage sliced thin then chopped into bite-size pieces
½ tsp of bacon flavored bits
Salt and a dash of Cayenne pepper to taste

In your favorite pan, melt the butter over low heat then add the onion, green peppers, and carrots. Sauté the onion, green pepper, and carrots together until the onion looks transparent and the carrots are tender. Add the cabbage, salt, and Cayenne pepper.

Simmer for 10 to 15 minutes to allow the flavors to blend.

The original recipe calls for real bacon, but if you use the bacon bits instead, it will give you the same taste without the added fat and calories. Makes approximately four servings.

Marta Stephens, award-winning author of The Sam Harper Crime Mysteries: The Devil Can Wait and Silenced Cry.
www.martastephens-author.com
http://mstephens-musings.blogspot.com
http://murderby4.blogspot.com
http://novelworks2.blogspot.com
http://samharpercrimescene.blogspot.com

Murder By Potato

Ingredients:

4 potatoes, sliced 1/8" thick
4 carrots, sliced lengthwise
1 onion, sliced
¼ cup Parmesan cheese
1 tsp garlic powder
½ cup butter
salt and pepper to taste
4 large pieces of aluminum foil

Divide vegetable ingredients and place on the four pieces of aluminum foil.

Sprinkle each with 1 Tbsp Parmesan cheese, ¼ tsp garlic powder, salt, and pepper to taste.

Place 2 Tbsp butter on top. Seal each package tightly at the top and sides. Heat oven to 375° F.

Bake for 25 minutes, then turn over and bake for another 25 minutes or until fork tender. Serves four.

Susanne Marie Knight, author of *Tainted Tea For Two*.
www.susanneknight.com
http://www.uncialpress.com

Nut-Stuffed Acorn Squash

Ingredients:

1 medium acorn squash (summer squash)
½ cup walnuts
½ cup blanched, skinned almonds
1 large onion
1 clove garlic
4 Tbsp oil
¾ cup whole grain breadcrumbs
2 Tbsp chopped parsley
1 Tbsp chopped thyme
1 egg, beaten
Juice and grated rind from one lemon

Preheat oven to 400° F.

Cut top off the squash to make a lid. Scoop out seeds from both lid and body of squash.
Fill large saucepan half full of water. Bring to boil.
Put in both squash and lid. Simmer for 5 minutes. Drain well.
Grind almonds and walnuts in blender.
Finely chop onions and garlic.
Heat oil in frying pan on low heat. Mix onion and garlic. Cook till soft. Remove pan from heat. Mix in breadcrumbs, nuts, herbs, lemon rind, juice, and egg.
Fill squash with the stuffing. Replace lid and secure with toothpicks.
Lightly butter a large casserole, or use non-stick spray. Arrange stuffed squash. Cover and bake 1 hour.

Mary Deal, author of *River Bones*.
www.WriteAnyGenre.com

Pop-Eyed Spinach Pie

Ingredients:

2 – 10 oz packages of fresh spinach
1 – 8 oz package cream cheese, softened
¼ cup sour cream
1 Tbsp minced garlic
¼ tsp salt
¼ tsp pepper
2 deep pie shells, thawed
Egg wash, optional

Boil spinach just long enough to make it limp. Drain and squeeze out remaining water.

In medium bowl, stir together cream cheese, sour cream, garlic, salt, and pepper. Add spinach. Use hands to get mixture distributed evenly. Pour into pie shell. Add top pie crust and slit. Brush top with egg wash if desired. Bake at 425° F for 20 to 25 minutes. Serve warm. (Best if refrigerated overnight and then sliced and warmed.)

Susan Whitfield, author of the award-winning Logan Hunter Mystery Series; *Genesis Beach, Just North of Luck, Hell Swamp,* and *Sin Creek.*
www.susanwhitfieldonline.com
www.susanwhitfield.blogspot.com
www.twitter.com/swhitfield

Shredded Apple Raisin Cole Slaw

Ingredients:

1 head cabbage shredded
2 Gala or Red Delicious apples, peeled and cubed
¼ cup raisins

Dressing:
½ cup low-fat mayonnaise
1 Tbsp apple cider vinegar
2 Tbsp milk
2 to 4 packets artificial sweetener or 1 to 2 Tbsp sugar

Peel and cube apples and toss with 1 Tbsp lemon juice to prevent browning. Add raisins and shredded cabbage then toss with dressing. Refrigerate for 2 hours before serving.

Caitlyn Hunter, author of *The Secret Life of Alice Smitty* in an L&L Dreamspell anthology.
http://caitlynhunter.com

Sliced Sweet Potato Apple Bake

Ingredients:

2 to 3 moderately sized sweet potatoes
About ¼ cup of brown sugar (depending how sweet you like your vegetables)
1 large granny smith apple (or other tart apple) chopped
1 to 2 Tbsp of butter

Peel and slice the sweet potatoes. Add one layer of sweet potato slices to the bottom of an 8 to 10 inch casserole dish. Dot these slices with butter and sprinkle some of the brown sugar and some of the chopped apples over the top. Add another layer of sweet potatoes, butter dots, brown sugar sprinkles, and chopped apple. Do this repeatedly until you've used up the sweet potatoes. Then cover the dish and place into the oven at 350° F for 45 minutes to an hour (depending how thick your slices are). It's done when the potatoes poke through easily with a fork.
Makes 4 servings.

Jodi Diederrich, author of *Hiram's Rock* in an L&L Dreamspell anthology.
www.jodidiederrich.com

Smashed Yams

Ingredients:

Yams (I prefer Red Garnet)
Sour cream (fat-free works just as well)
Toasted walnut halves

Prick yams, wrap in paper towels, and cook in microwave until soft when squeezed. (I do them one by one—a middle-sized yam takes about 3 minutes on high, turn over, another 2 minutes on high.) Bake in oven if you prefer.
Cut in half to let steam escape. When cool enough to handle, peel, then mash with potato masher. They're better not completely smooth but don't leave big lumps.
Add about ¼ cup of sour cream per 2 cups of mashed yams, more or less to taste, and mix thoroughly.
Put in ovenproof casserole, smooth top, decorate with walnut halves.
Covered, this can be kept hot or reheated in the oven or microwave.

Carola Dunn, author of *A Colourful Death* (2010) and The Daisy Dalrymple Mysteries.
http://CarolaDunn.weebly.com

Stolen Greens and Bacon

Ingredients:

1 bunch Kale, Swiss chard, or Beet Greens
2 to 3 slices bacon, chopped
1 Tbsp cider vinegar (to taste)
¼ to ½ tsp black pepper

Wash greens thoroughly and remove stems.
Add chopped bacon to large Dutch oven and cook until nearly crisp.
Add wet greens, vinegar, and pepper to Dutch oven and cover.
Stir frequently, closing lid between stirs.
When greens are completely wilted, remove to cutting board and chop with large knife.

Harol Marshall, author of *Holy Death and A Corpse for Cuamantla*.
www.harolmarshall.com

Index of Contributing Authors

Front Cover Photo Key:
1. Mushrooms to Die For
2. Mad Russian Tea
3. Black Eyed Salad
4. Clandestine Cheese Puffs
5. Crazy Pumpkin Crisp

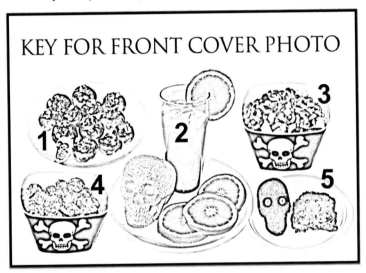

KEY FOR FRONT COVER PHOTO

Back Cover Photo Key:
1. Howling Hot Apple Crisp
2. Deadly Chocolate Pudding Cake
3. Grave Robber's Coffee Mix
4. Kate's Working Mom Pizza
5. Breakfast Before Mayhem
6. Potent Vegetarian Taco Soup
7. Wacky Zucchini Bread
8. Murder by Potato
9. Meat Cleaver's Taco Dip
10. Vicious Vegetarian Lasagna
11. Criminal Chicken Chili Casserole
12. Mean McLean's Famous Mac 'N Cheese

KEY FOR BACK COVER PHOTO

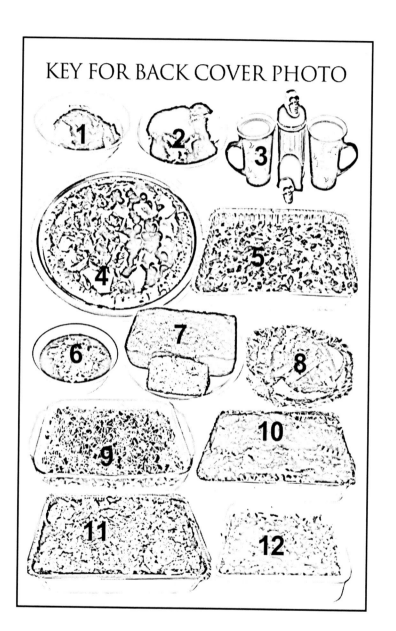